Eight Trails

Eight Trails

Ancient Maps for Life's Wilderness

BY JOANNE M. SWENSON

WIPF & STOCK · Eugene, Oregon

EIGHT TRAILS
Ancient Maps for Life's Wilderness

Copyright © 2025 Joanne M. Swenson. All rights reserved. Except for brief quotations in critical publications or reviews, no part of this book may be reproduced in any manner without prior written permission from the publisher. Write: Permissions, Wipf and Stock Publishers, 199 W. 8th Ave., Suite 3, Eugene, OR 97401.

Wipf & Stock
An Imprint of Wipf and Stock Publishers
199 W. 8th Ave., Suite 3
Eugene, OR 97401

www.wipfandstock.com

PAPERBACK ISBN: 979-8-3852-4956-5
HARDCOVER ISBN: 979-8-3852-4957-2
EBOOK ISBN: 979-8-3852-4958-9

11/03/25

Scripture quotations marked (NIV) taken from The Holy Bible, New International Version®, NIV®. Copyright © 1973, 1978, 1984, 2011 by Biblica, Inc. Used with permission of Zondervan. All rights reserved worldwide. www.zondervan.com.

Scripture quotations marked (NRSVUE) are taken from the New Revised Standard Version Updated Edition. Copyright © 2021 National Council of Churches of Christ in the United States of America. Used by permission. All rights reserved worldwide.

Scripture quotations marked (ESV) are from The ESV® Bible (The Holy Bible, English Standard Version®), © 2001 by Crossway, a publishing ministry of Good News Publishers. Used by permission. All rights reserved.

Scripture quotations marked (KJV) are from The Authorized (King James) Version. Rights in the Authorized Version in the United Kingdom are vested in the Crown. Reproduced by permission of the Crown's patentee, Cambridge University Press.

Scripture quotations marked (NASB) taken from the (NASB®) New American Standard Bible®, Copyright © 1960, 1971, 1977 by The Lockman Foundation. Used by permission. All rights reserved. lockman.org.

Scripture quotations marked (NLT) are taken from the Holy Bible, New Living Translation, copyright ©1996, 2004, 2015 by Tyndale House Foundation. Used by permission of Tyndale House Publishers, Carol Stream, Illinois 60188. All rights reserved.

For my children, to follow trails higher than mine

Contents

*Preface: What Trail Map Are You Using?
    Invitation to Eight Trails | ix*

Acknowledgments | xi

Introduction | 1

Chapter 1   The Trail of Life Rhythms | 11
Chapter 2   The Trail of Reverence Before *The More* | 20
Chapter 3   The Trail of Revelation | 29
Chapter 4   The Trail of Resilience | 35
Chapter 5   The Trail of Relationship | 44
Chapter 6   The Trail of Regulation | 54
Chapter 7   The Trail of Repentance | 62
Chapter 8   The Trail of Resurrection | 70
Chapter 9   Conclusion | 81

Bibliography | 93

Preface

What Trail Map Are You Using? Invitation to Eight Trails

Puzzled by many religious beliefs, I was driven to understand religion, especially my own, Christianity. This question has inspired me since my teens, researching, teaching, and participating in faith communities, university classrooms, and in the solitude of my faith.

Here's where I'm at right now.

Religious beliefs are like maps; they are symbolic guides to help us venture into the unknown—that is, our everyday life.

But just like any map, you need to be shown how to use it. After all, what map looks like the terrain it symbolizes? You need a more experienced traveler to show you how to read its symbols.

Inspired by the true story of a young family lost in a wintry mountain wilderness, I reflect on how religious symbols can guide us on our wilderness trails.

These are the trails we'll consider:

1. The Trail of Life Rhythms
2. The Trail of Reverence Before *The More*
3. The Trail of Revelation
4. The Trail of Resilience

Preface

5. The Trail of Relationship
6. The Trail of Regulation
7. The Trail of Repentance
8. The Trail of Resurrection

These can be thought of as the Eight Trails, eight paths for living with joy, purpose, and strength. This book explores the power of religious symbols to guide us through life's wilderness.

Eight Trails was written for my own young adult kids. But if you have questions about religion, it's for you as well.

Acknowledgments

I am grateful to Susan Tetrick of Portland, Oregon, my encourager and editor for the past year. Even more, Susan has been a true friend for almost a quarter century, and a wise guide through my joys and challenges. Thank you, Lord, for bringing Susan and me together!

Introduction

THE BREAKING NEWS

Do you remember when we heard the breaking news?

We were wrapping Christmas presents at Grandma's where the TV was always droning. But this broadcast caught our attention. A San Francisco family—two parents and their young children—was missing in the Oregon wilderness.

It was 2006 and, as grade-schoolers, you already loved Oregon's forests from happy times of canoeing, hiking—even a few overnights, high in a fire tower. But now James and Kati Kim were not on a happy holiday. They and their little girls, a four-year-old and an eight-month-old baby, were missing somewhere in Oregon's vast Siskiyou wilderness in the fearsome cold of December.

MAPS MISUNDERSTOOD

James Kim knew his way around digital maps and computer codes. He was a rising star at CNET, researching and reviewing the latest consumer technology. But his high-tech world did not prepare him to understand that most ancient symbol—a paper map of roads and rivers.

Friends think the Kim family probably began their trip guided by directions from MapQuest or Google. This would be the tool of choice for such digital early adopters. But in those first years of development, digital maps were sometimes faulty. So, at some point in their journey, James and Kati had purchased a paper road map to supplement their virtual one.

Now, after they missed a crucial turn, they pulled out that paper map. It showed a forest service road, Bear Camp Road—a thin black line that seemed to promise a speedy return to their route toward the Oregon coast.

Yet, they missed the paper map's footnote about Bear Camp Road: *"Road closed in winter."*[1]

What happened? Maybe James and Kati were reading from the car's dim light. Maybe they missed the map's footnote symbol.

It would become a fatal oversight.

The Kims kept driving toward peril until deep snow halted any possible movement forward—or back. They were trapped in Bear Camp Road's snow and darkness. Resigned to their impasse, they settled in for the night, turning the engine off and on to stay warm, trying conserve their fuel.

The Kims were not able to use their maps. First, their digital map failed them. Second, while they had an accurate paper map, they didn't read it carefully.

MAPS OF FAITH

This book is dedicated to helping you use a map through your own wilderness. And although I am speaking especially to my own

---

1. Suo et al., "Conflicts."

INTRODUCTION

adult kids, this book is concerned, as well, with your friends and all those at a crucial juncture in life.

You're in your late twenties with life-altering choices ahead: where to live, what is your life's calling, and with whom will you partner for friendship and family. These choices are like the wilderness trails you have long explored and loved. And you've always accepted the trail's risk and uncertainty for its promise of joy and beauty.

Here's my hope for you: as you choose your wilderness trails, I invite you to reconsider the maps provided by the world's great faiths. I'll ask you to rethink religion as a powerful map—not a collection of mythologies from a misty past, but powerfully relevant for your daily reality, orienting you to what's real.

Like a map.

MAPS FOR MOVING AHEAD

This idea of religion as a series of maps comes from my mentor, the late Harvard professor Gordon Kaufman. Dr. Kaufman used the metaphor of maps to describe how religion is used by its believers.

> Charts and models are always our constructions of a reality which is too immense, or otherwise inaccessible, to grasp without their aid. . . . Whether this accurately represents the "actual structure" . . . no one can say; and it really does not matter at all. The map is a good one *if it enables us to get where we are trying to go*.[2]

Religion's enduring power lies in its effectiveness in getting us where we're trying to go as we face the vast unknown of our lives.

A map.

The first maps you learned to use were in grade school, those flour-and-salt maps of our state's starring features. From these you learned the locations of the Deschutes and Willamette Rivers, the glorious shape of Mount Hood, the expanse of Oregon's high desert, the depth of Crater Lake.

---

2. Kaufman, *Essay on Theological Method*, 45; emphasis added.

But even at that young age, you understood those maps worked as models. As a flour-and-salt model, your Crater Lake wasn't meant to hold water—your map would have turned to mush!

Already at that grade school age, you were learning the unique challenge of maps: they depict something that is certainly real, but they don't look like the reality they depict! That's okay—that's how they work. As Professor Kaufman said, "The map is a good one if it enables us to get where we are trying to go."

MAP MENTORS

Maps are symbols for something real. Yet because they aren't photographic images but complex symbols, you need some help to use them.

Remember the time when you were hiking in the sun-drenched Glen Canyon National Recreation Area? You and your friends were counting on getting down the canyon walls to cool off in the Colorado River. In fact, you knew about that river by seeing numerous photos. But those realistic photos were useless for what you had to do next.

As you approached the canyon walls, they were too steep to descend. Fortunately, one of your friends was an outdoor expert from his years working for the Department of Natural Resources. He pulled out a specialized paper map—a topographic map. By reading its contour lines, he determined exactly where you could descend.

You made your way down to the water and splashed around with joy.

The topo map was ideal for guiding your way to water. But you needed your friend's expertise, as well.

INTRODUCTION

MISUNDERSTANDING MAPS?

Now you read a variety of maps—the latest ones are special rock climbing maps with difficulty numbers, and bolts required, and where there's troublesome shade. These maps take decoding skills you learned from fellow adventurers.

But think about this: What if you headed out to climb and discarded your rock climbing map because it didn't look like the wall you faced? You didn't understand its code? You didn't have someone to show you how to use its rock climbing symbols?

Dumb, huh?

Well, let's consider religion. Did you participate long enough in a faith community to learn to read its maps? *Could it be that you discarded centuries of wisdom, strength, and inspiration—centuries of maps—before you learned to read them?*

You left church as a teenager, thinking, "Religion is about these strange, unbelievable things! God on a throne, angels in heaven, the Red Sea parted, and the Jordan River held back! And what about that wandering sage who changes water to wine and heals with a word or a touch? I look around the world I live in, and there's *nothing* that looks like that!"

THE PRIMARY FOCUS IS THE FUTURE

But maps don't look like or replicate reality, so you need help in using them. Whether progressive or deeply conservative, religious folks learn to read their maps through participation in a faith community. They are organically tutored through hearing sermons, participating in Bible studies, reading inspirational books, singing music, and joining in rituals.

And yes, I know, we have some dear friends who say that the Bible's stories do look like reality—that these stories are historically true or will one day be vindicated by science.

We do have friends who insist that Noah's ark is somewhere in Turkey, waiting to be dug up!

But don't be so quick to dismiss them or their faith. For if you observe closely what they're up to, their *primary* focus is not on some unbelievable past and trying to prove it to you. Their real focus is on the *future*. They're trying to discern how to shape their lives in ways that bless our world.[3]

They use their sacred symbols as maps that guide their way through this wilderness.

THE MAP OF GOD

One of the most important maps we'll need is that of our overall world—the cosmos! This is the vast *mystery* in which we dwell yet take for granted every day. To put our feet on the ground each morning as we get out of bed, we implicitly trust a map.

Science provides one kind of map for this world of floorboards and bedrooms. Science, using its tools of cause and effect, can work out the molecular structure of wood, the bearing loads for floors, predictions about the weather outside.

Those maps are helpful, but not enough.

Humans need purpose and value and hope to swing their legs out of bed and stand. We need a sense that this world has meaning for us. We need an overall picture of the *moral dimensions* of the cosmos.

We find that picture in the map of "God." Every great world religion, in its own distinguishing way, offers a map of the overall context in which we live. And each religion calls that mystery, that vast and limitless context, by a sacred name: the Divine, Nirvana, the Tao, Yahweh, Brahma, Ahura Mazda, Allah, Christ.

These names all function to say that the cosmos is imbued with *this* distinctive personality, *this* compelling character. You can count on *this* when your feet hit the floorboards.

Those names aren't interchangeable. They suggest vastly different tones or atmospheres to this mystery in which we dwell.

---

3. Theologian Dorothy Bass's work has long emphasized that the practices of faith are more significant in religious life than doctrine or beliefs. See her influential book, *Practicing Our Faith: A Way of Life for a Searching People*.

Introduction

Although there is tremendous overlap in values between religious faiths, each has a distinctive spirit. Each has a distinctive way of picturing "home" that shapes the energies and hopes of its followers.

These aren't maps of spatial quality but of the world's spiritual quality. In that way, the symbol "God" is the greatest of maps, giving an overall spirit to our cosmic home.

In my own faith, Christianity, we understand this mystery as *Father*—creative, personal, shining in beauty. So we sing,

> This is my Father's world:
> I rest me in the thought
> Of rocks and trees, of skies and seas—
> His hand the wonders wrought.
> . . . .
> This is my Father's world:
> He shines in all that's fair;
> In the rustling grass I hear Him pass,
> He speaks to me everywhere.

And when evil and tragedy seem to contradict the world of "My Father," this hymn insists,

> This is my Father's world:
> O let me ne'er forget
> That though the wrong seems oft so strong,
> God is the Ruler yet.
> This is my Father's world:
> Why should my heart be sad?
> The Lord is king: 'let the heavens ring!
> God reigns; let earth be glad![4]

That vision of God shapes the steps of those who sing this song. Even in the face of life's tragedies and injustice, those who follow the map of "my Father" move ahead in confidence.

---

4. Babcock, "This Is My Father's World," stanzas 1–3.

WHAT'S THIS BOOK ABOUT?

I hope by now you understand that maps are meant to be used! Maps of faith are not hung on a wall for decor. No, maps of faith are taken out on the trail and put to work in life's wilderness.

So, pay attention to how religious people *use* their stories. They are used to discern patterns—hiking trails, if you will—to guide us through our wilderness. These stories can empower, encourage, and even restrain where we need to be checked and held back.

In the new year ahead, we'll encounter places where we need caution, stops for marveling in joy, speed zones that demand self-regulation, and rest stops to renew our spirit. These can be thought of as the Eight Trails, eight paths for living with joy, purpose, and strength.

There's nothing specific to a religion, or a denomination, in these eight trails—or even religion in general. These are widely desired paths of life, whether or not you're religious. And you can certainly try to hike each trail without a religious map.

But I will try to persuade you that religious maps provide essential, life-giving guidance. The trail goes better with maps based on something *more*. That *more* can be called "God."

RELIGION—MINE OR THINE?

Most of the world's great religious traditions have thought deeply about these trails and have profound resources to help your progress on them.

While I, thus, have spoken generally about "religions," my own religion has always been Christianity, and so I know it best. I can't help but interpret other religions through my Christian eyes, as well.

But I aim to commend not so much a specific religion but a way of understanding all religions as powerfully orienting maps. The accent note is not on any religion's *accuracy* about its sacred

INTRODUCTION

events or beings, its long-past history, or its heavenly realms. Rather, the accent is on *activation*.

Does this religious map activate a life lived fully and generously?

As a Christian who has used its maps all my life, I enthusiastically commend Christian maps. As I mature and face my own wilderness (you kids know!), I have grown in awe at the profundity, sustaining power, and sublime beauty of Jesus and his teachings.

In addition, I have taught Islam, Buddhism, Daoism, etc. in my work as a professor. I am moved by their ancient wisdom and how they expand my Christian views. I am convinced that when their own maps are interpreted by wise and bold believers, they lead to living water that flows in with other faiths. They can produce lives dedicated to caring for the weak, seeking justice for the oppressed and truth for the searcher, reconciliation with enemies, self-restraint in our behavior, and sharing our wealth with others.

When I've taught world religions, frankly, it's like "Students, this week it's Hinduism; next week it's Buddhism," etc. But I gave my students a semester-long homework assignment that many say changed their lives. I asked them to "try out" that week's religion, as though they were a new convert; reflect on how that religious tradition changes their long-term outlook and immediate, daily habits; and especially, decide which can truly guide them in the challenges of their lives. Which will help them live with integrity, face their losses, confront their lapses, and walk with hope when life seems too hard?

I challenged them: *test the map*.

As Jesus himself said to those who first wondered about following him, "Come and see" (John 1:39 NRSVUE).

THE WAY AHEAD

Did you toss aside religion before you learned to read its maps? Did you toss it aside as false, irrelevant, even oppressive?

Can you return to those maps and reassess them?

And as we smooth out those rumpled maps, we'll return to the story of the Kim Family. They may have failed to read their maps of turnoffs and closed roads, but so, too, have we. Each day and dilemma of their journey is also experienced by us.

    Let's begin with a trail that is as ordinary and universal as checking the clock: finding a rhythm by which to live.

Chapter 1

The Trail of Life Rhythms

SEEKING REST

The Kims were on holiday break, exhaling from busy lives as professionals and parents.

James was in demand as a CNET TV personality and technology consultant. New products and innovations required his attention each day. Kati managed two San Francisco boutiques: a continual juggle of people, merchandise, and the physical plant. But these stores, so beloved by neighbors and tourists, were her rich reward. Adding to their responsibilities, the Kims had welcomed a new baby to the family seven months ago, and Kati was committed to nursing her.

The Kims, as we might guess, were grateful for the pause provided by Thanksgiving. But that pause began with bustle. First, they drove their Saab wagon up to Seattle to enjoy Thanksgiving with James's aunt and uncle. Then they headed south to Portland to visit Kati's friends, adding an excursion to explore Portland's special shops.

Finally, they loaded the girls into the wagon and began driving down Interstate 5, toward Oregon's famed forest hideaway, the Tu Tu'Tun Lodge. There they would finally have that holiday pause.

Their drive began Friday afternoon, November 26.[1]

THE CADENCES OF CULTURE

The Kims were following a map of rhythm, the cadences of culture—shared rhythms that shape the energy of work, school, and life.

Here's something you kids and I can all agree on: our need for holidays and celebrations!

You're experts, in fact, on celebration. Although I wasn't there to witness, I heard about those campus-wide, end-of-term celebrations, with music, dancing, and more. (I'll never forget when you explained the Cornell meaning of "darties"—parties that start in the daytime.)

College life, especially, relies on such cadences to sustain the souls of its students. Weeks of dreary winter weather, intense preparations for crucial tests, grueling writing of papers, and anxious days of exams demand a final celebration.

Before you left home for college, your most constant cadence was our family supper. No matter how busy or tired, we gathered around the table Dad would set with place mats and cloth napkins. Candles were lit and grace was said, a reminder that this time was special. The clink of forks, the hum of shared stories, the simple presence of each other—this ritual expressed, "Now, we stop, we've worked enough, all we need is here."

---

1. Austin and Larabee, "On the Road."

The Trail of Life Rhythms

You can see that same cadence in our larger culture and the weeks leading up to Christmas. Four weeks of lists, errands, decorating, and parties build to a frenetic crescendo. But then at sunset on Christmas Eve, there's a clear call to halt this hectic pace. The true Christmas has begun.

And, for many, the climax of this busy season comes with a celebration of silence—the spreading of candlelight in a darkened, hushed church—then "Silent Night" is sung. Even the most secular and cynical want to experience the precious hours of Christmas just like this, lost in wonder, beauty, and joy.

Can you imagine a life without these cadences? Our days would just grind on without any texture or identity. But holidays wrap our lives with gilded frames of meaning. These frames hold time and proclaim, "Now—your work is over!" "Now—here's extraordinary time!" "Now—here is your very life, framed so you can feel and remember it."

We create a chapter book of our lives through such cadences. Our lives gain shape and direction through these cultural rhythms. But to apprehend their meaning, we must pause to truly see. We must rest in the moment. As we sing on Christmas Eve, almost admonishing ourselves, "Sleep in heavenly peace, / sleep in heavenly peace."[2]

RELIGIOUS REST

The cadences of high holidays like Easter, Thanksgiving, and Christmas have their origins in religion, obviously.

But does religion have anything to do with basic, *bodily* rest? Yes.

Religion has long cared about rest—and not just how, but who gets rest.

In cultures shaped by Jewish-Christian traditions, the weekly rest day has been called "Sabbath" (thus, we have "sabbatical").

---

2. Mohr, "Silent Night," stanza 1.

Sabbath practices emerged from ancient Scripture obliging all to refrain from work. Exodus 20 describes its dimensions:

> Remember the Sabbath day and keep it holy. Six days you shall labor and do all your work. But the seventh day is a Sabbath to the LORD your God; you shall not do any work—you, your son or your daughter, your male or female slave, your livestock, or the alien resident in your towns. For in six days, the LORD made heaven and earth, the sea, and all that is in them, but rested the seventh day; therefore the LORD blessed the Sabbath day and consecrated it. (Exod 20:8–11 NRSVUE)

What is so interesting about this obligation is that the Jewish people describe this law as decreed by God amid an urgent journey. The Jews are fleeing enslavement from the Egyptians and wandering in the wilderness (wilderness, again!) in search of the promised land. This is no time for them to delay or linger. Yet, rather than advising them to keep on pushing forward, God commands them to stop and rest—one full day each week.

And on that day, they were not even to labor for bread. On the eve of the Sabbath, God bestowed a double supply of miraculous bread, which rained down from the sky, called "manna." They could trust in God's provision and celebrate one full day each week. They were called to set aside worry and live in the present with thanks.

It's a great story, full of miracles and wonder. But doesn't it also sound oddly real—even *scientific*?

Recent research on rest and productivity has affirmed the wisdom of these ancient traditions of breaking up intense, essential work with protected periods of rest. And history describes how innovative and brilliant leaders have relied on naps, walks, and meditation to sustain their productivity.

But there is deeper and surprising wisdom in the ancient practice of Sabbath. Sabbath wasn't just about self-care—it was a form of justice. Did you notice who was to rest in that Exodus reading?

The Trail of Life Rhythms

You shall not do any work—you, your son or your daughter, your male or female slave, your livestock, or the alien resident in your towns. (Exod 20:10 NRSVUE)

The Hebrew people were *obliged* to stop work—not only for their own rest but especially to provide rest for the most subjugated, invisible, and voiceless of workers: children caring for aging parents without recognition, slaves toiling under a harsh master, the easily exploited "alien" or outsider, and even mute, domestic animals.

All were entitled to Sabbath rest. Sabbath was a day when all were treated equally, accorded the dignity of being a creation of God.

The Exodus story of Sabbath rest seems to occur in some mythical past. But we can use it to shape our path now. Sabbath does this in two ways:

1. It teaches us to regard each other—and even our animals—with dignity and care, allowing them to rest.

2. It teaches that our lives are more than labor, cogs in some impersonal machine, living under the thumb of others. No, we are so beloved and cared for by God that he[3] provides what we need for that one day each week.

When we begin to see and act this way on the Sabbath, it spills over into the other six days. This map truly shapes our path.

REST WITHOUT RELIGION?

What about our modern, secularized Sabbath?

---

3. Of course, God doesn't have a gender, but I'll occasionally use the pronoun, "he" or "his" to refer to God. In this book, I can't revisit all the scholarship and popular debate about gendering God. What matters in this issue (and all other religious talk) is *how do we read this map?* If people read male pronouns or metaphors for God as a reason to elevate men over women, denying women autonomy and avenues of service, that's an error in map reading. A minor detail—masculinity—is obscuring the bigger trail. It will, inevitably, lead to dead ends.

On any Sunday in any town, you can see people wearying themselves with errands, yard and house upkeep. Low-wage workers continue to toil, ringing up your groceries or filling your brunch orders while you hardly notice, let alone wonder about the families they can't enjoy on this day. High-wage workers often feel compelled to return to a quiet office to catch up on pressing work.

And yes, most workers will get a day or two off in a seven day cycle. But we're all on our own to create our Sabbath—a private, individual rest. There is no civic, communal celebration that all enjoy together. No spirit gilds an entire community in a glow of rest. Missing is a sense of communal, shared dignity, enjoyed by all because they are created in the image of God—a God who even rests!

BUT REALLY? GOD NAPS?

Yes, this Exodus story claims God rests. "For in six days, the LORD made heaven and earth, the sea, and all that is in them, but rested the seventh day" (Exod 20:11 NRSVUE).

God's resting is given as the rationale for our human resting. All people and animals are called to imitate God in his action of rest! All are esteemed as worthy to model their lives after God's.

Now we've waded deep into religion. Now we're introducing religious language that goes way past the scientific view of biological rest. Exodus recalls the Genesis story that portrays God as a real, walking being who enjoys the garden of Eden and, indeed, as someone who rests!

What should you do, my skeptical kids, about this stuff?

We won't see this strolling God through cosmic telescopes. We certainly won't catch him napping!

Well, let's remember our opening thesis: religious claims should be read as *maps*. *These maps are created for orientation, to figure out what we should do.* And, if you read this Exodus story about God carefully, you find that's exactly what's going on.

Exodus says, because God rests, *therefore* we should rest.

This image of a God who rests truly guides *human* action.

The upshot of this story is *not* that we should investigate questions like, "Who is God that he must rest?" or "If God rests, does that mean eternity is changeable?" or "What about those other Bible verses that say, 'God never slumbers nor sleeps'?"

And on and on.

No, the upshot is on what *we* should do. This claim about God boomerangs back to us, *regulating* our behavior. The great Enlightenment philosopher Immanuel Kant was the first to notice this crucial "regulative" dynamic of our claims about God. What religious people do with these claims for God is to turn the claim back to themselves, to "regulate" themselves—how *they* think and act.

These stories and theological claims guide human living.

The philosopher Don Cupitt teaches at the University of Cambridge and is also an Anglican priest. When he recites the Christian creed (a statement with many claims about God), he understands it this way: "When I say the Creed, I regard it not as giving me *supernatural* information, but it's showing me a way to walk."

The creed becomes a map for us.

And remember this: maps don't look exactly like what they represent. So, this map portrays a God who naps; does such an "object" exist—a napping God? How could we know? But it doesn't matter. This story map portrays something profoundly real for our lives.

THE MAP OF SABBATH

This Sabbath map is a powerful guide for sustaining our life and others, especially in the face of family responsibilities, work pressures, and financial anxieties. Even more, this Sabbath map guides us to experience this day with a sense of our ultimate worth. In Sabbath, we experience our divine dignity, and then share that dignity with others. And this Sabbath way of experiencing life flows into our other days.

But what about all the other stuff in these Sabbath laws and stories? Granted, these stories contain ancient features that aren't a part of our lives—laws about cooking fires, goats and sheep, looms for making cloth.

We're going to have to do some reinterpretation of these laws.

But that reinterpretation actually doesn't take us away from religion or diminish its power. Rather, reinterpretation puts us in a long line of devout thinkers who have continually rethought how to keep Sabbath in the face of new circumstances. (No cooking on the Sabbath? Okay, but does microwave reheating count as cooking? No carrying a burden on the Sabbath. Okay, but can't a wheelchair be pushed to synagogue?)

Religious communities have always had circles of devout thinkers and debaters who reinterpret the claims of faith. Jesus, indeed, was part of that long line of thinkers when he rejected oppressive Sabbath laws, saying, "The sabbath was made for man, and not man for the sabbath" (Mark 2:27).

YOUR RATIONAL DECISION ABOUT LIFE'S RHYTHM

This may make you uneasy and cause you to say, "Hey, can't I have my rest and holidays and Christmas carols without all this 'God stuff'?"

Yes, you can.

But look at the deeper power of the religious map.

The Sabbath guides us to affirm the dignity of others—even the lowliest and laboring of animals. We are called to rest and celebrate as a high command from heaven that no one should violate, especially against others.

And recognizing these religious rhythms gives *your* life more dignity. This religious map says, "We are not just isolated human beings trying to survive, to get through each day in a blur of joyless toil. No! Our worth is based on a higher power no human can take away. And we are called to pace our lives according to the very rhythms of this higher power. We rest and celebrate with God because 'the Lord rested on the seventh day.'"

WHAT'S NEXT?

We've started with something obviously "real," an aspect of life biological: the human need for rest. But we've gone way past the biological and onto the spiritual. We've begun to examine the differences between understanding rest without religion and understanding it from a religious perspective of shared dignity and sacred rhythm.

And I've begun to encourage you to think more deeply about religion—not as discredited pseudoscience or a series of false facts, but as a deeply symbolic map. Maps may not look like what they depict, but dismiss them at your peril. You can lose your way in the wilderness.

The next trail also addresses something real and universal—our awestruck wonder before the sheer miracle of life. While one need not be religious to experience that awe, I'll frame this next topic with a spiritual word—that word is "reverence."

CHAPTER 2

The Trail of Reverence Before The More

SEEKING AWE

The Kims were on their way to a glorious spot in the Siskiyou Forest—the *Tu Tu'Tun Lodge*.

Its seclusion guarantees you an astonishing night of stargazing, with hardly a light to obscure the stars' glimmer. Outside your cabin door, the lapping sounds of the Rogue River invite your contemplation. And just a short drive away, at Gold Beach, the Kims would have exalted in the ocean's immensity.

Kids, you understand what the Kims were seeking—wonder and awe! Beneath stars only disclosed in darkest wilderness, you discovered wonder. You've set up your tents beside singing rivers,

The Trail of Reverence Before The More

merging into their music. And to sense the ocean's infinity, you never tired of that serpentine drive to Cannon Beach.

I remember awe's quiet arrival on a mother-daughter outing. Siri, you were about eleven, and we were alone in a primitive cabin at a Girl Scout camp. Cocooned in our sleeping bags, the night had long settled in when you awoke me. Your voice was trembling, afraid of the strange noises outside.

"Mama, what is that sound?"

"Crickets," I whispered.

The walls of our suburban house had always muffled nature's songs. But out here in our wilderness cabin, its songs trilled through the cabin's plank walls—symphonic, relentless, alive.

You were amazed. Amazed that you'd lived eleven summers and somehow missed the crickets. That night, we listened in reverence.

I remember a different kind of lesson about reverence from Erik's Boy Scout trip to the Oregon Coast. The campsite was nestled near the ocean, and you could hear the crash of waves just beyond the trees. For most of the time, however, the focus was on fulfilling badge requirements. The boys and their leaders sat hunched over merit badge books, practicing knots and studying fire-building techniques. The natural beauty of the coast—the shimmering water, the scent of the salt air, the slow dance of the tide—was largely ignored.

There was only one afternoon set aside for exploring the tidal pools. That glimpse into the mysterious underwater world—starfish clinging to rocks, anemones blooming beneath the surface—was magical. Erik, you were so taken by it all, full of questions and awe.

That desire for awe touches us all. Some make the hard journey to the Arctic Circle to behold the aurora borealis. Some wait quietly in the predawn chill of Nebraska to witness thousands of sandhill cranes lifting off at sunrise. Some will dive into the waters of Curaçao to be enveloped by its iridescent fish.

But one doesn't need to travel to experience that awe. You might be struck by it as you walk across a quiet, snow-covered city park, like American philosopher Ralph Waldo Emerson: "Crossing a bare common, in snow puddles, at twilight, under a clouded sky, without having in my thoughts any occurrence of special good fortune, I have enjoyed a perfect exhilaration.... Standing on the bare ground, my head bathed by the blithe air, and uplifted into infinite space—all mean egotism vanishes.... I am nothing. I see all. The currents of the Universal Being circulate through me; I am part or parcel of God."[1]

I am nothing, but I see all! My small self is part of something so much more! The early twentieth-century philosopher William James used that very word "more" to describe religious experience. He observed that beneath all the variety of religious creeds and practices, there exists a widespread awareness that our most real selves are connected to a *more*: "He becomes conscious that higher part [of himself] is conterminous and continuous with a MORE of the same quality, which is operative in the universe outside of him."[2]

Philosophers have long pondered the human reaction to this "more," often using the term "The Sublime." The Sublime includes those experiences that overwhelm us with beauty, immensity, wonder.

But The Sublime isn't just a feature of external objects—it's something in us that is evoked by the object. *We* have the capacity to be moved by surpassing beauty, to grasp a miracle of grace, to be drawn to a beckoning mystery we can't comprehend but love to contemplate.

We are humbled by these encounters—we sense our own smallness in the face of these immense wonders. And this humbling is welcomed! We feel astonished gratitude that we are allowed to experience The Sublime.

---

1. Emerson, *Nature*, 4.
2. James, *Varieties*, 328; emphasis in original.

The Trail of Reverence Before The More

THE SUBLIME AND SCIENCE

Scientists themselves experience the emotions of The Sublime / The More amid their questions and discoveries. One of the twentieth century's greatest physicists, Richard Feynman, wrote of the rapture he regularly felt in his work: "Poets say science takes away from the beauty of the stars—mere globs of gas atoms. Nothing is 'mere.' I too can see the stars on a desert night and feel them. But do I see less or more? The vastness of the heavens stretches my imagination—stuck on this carousel my little eye can catch one-million-year-old light."[3]

These moments of astonished awe are common experiences among hikers, birders, and theoretical physicists! So, no surprise that such awe has become a subject itself for scientific understanding. Two social psychologists identified thousands of research subjects who had experienced this awe. However, their study went further and measured the impact of awe on those individuals. They found that those who experienced sublime awe were more willing to help a stranger, including sharing resources and sacrificing for another.

Why? In the researchers' words, "One answer is that awe imbues people with a different sense of themselves, one that is smaller, humbler, and part of something larger. Our research finds that even brief experiences of awe, such as being amid beautiful tall trees, lead people to feel less narcissistic and entitled and more attuned to the common humanity people share with one another."[4]

Notice how moral and even religious ideas are now entering into this very common and documentable experience?

- "... attuned to the common humanity people share"
- "... part of something larger"
- Reminding us of Emerson's words, "I am part or parcel of God"

---

3. Feynman, as quoted in Sykes, *No Ordinary Genius*, 17.
4. Piff and Keltner, "Why Do We Experience Awe?"

The Sublime pushes us past the language of ordinary realism. We are having an experience that many others share—it's public and even lends itself to photographs and scientific analysis. But it outstrips the language of analysis and documentation. Think of a group, analyzing the colors of the aurora borealis but also shivering together in wonder. Imagine those birders, counting sandhill cranes but also gasping in joy as they lift off.

Our realistic language and scientific analysis just can't do justice to this moment. We may whisper, "Ah, ah," we may tear up, we may fall to our knees in astonishment, or even stand tall to raise our arms in reverence.

Reverence? Now, that's a term with religious meaning. So, let's move past simple, secular language and give these moments a term that captures their spiritual significance. In these moments of *reverence*, we sense our connection to a grander, cosmic mystery.[5] As one philosopher observed, such moments bring us to a "deep conviction of a fundamental and indelible solidarity of life . . . an indestructible unity of life."[6]

CULTIVATING REVERENCE

The Sublime is simply ineffable, outstripping the powers of everyday language. Yet, it is experienced through the everyday realities of snowy nights, mountain hikes, even research in the lab. When we experience The More in material reality, we are experiencing that there is "more" to life *in this life*! Material reality itself offers us this more—if we're sensitive to this offering.

But how do we gain that sensitivity? How can we cultivate what one philosopher called "the sense and taste for the Infinite"?[7]

---

5. Philosopher Howard Wettstein argues that such awe is the basis for religious faith, not metaphysical doctrines. See his work, *The Significance of Religious Experience*.

6. Cassirer, *Essay on Man*, 82.

7. Used first by Friedrich Schleiermacher in his 1799 work, *On Religion: Speeches to Its Cultured Despisers*, 23.

THE TRAIL OF REVERENCE BEFORE THE MORE

The great religious traditions are in the very business of The More. Their stories, rituals, and special places cultivate within humans an expectation and awareness of The More. And notice this: these great traditions do not seal up The More in some special heaven, seen only by the "saved." No, they insist that The More dwells among us, beckoning and blessing us. As the Christian apostle Paul put it, "[God] is not far from any one of us. 'For in him we live and move and have our being'" (Acts 17:27–28 NIV).

The More / The Sublime is the awareness that here, in this world of sandhill cranes and snowy parks, starry nights and long days at the lab, we can experience that *something*, that More in whom "we live and move and have our being."

JESUS AS THE MORE

The great religious traditions also say that certain extraordinary human beings even manifest this "more." Let me speak to that experience as a Christian.

The Christian faith begins with a real, historical person—Jesus. But the first Christian community saw more in Jesus. Early Christians testified to that "more" in their biblical stories about Jesus. As they remembered Jesus and saw him through their Jewish traditions, their ideas about Jesus went far past mere historical fact. Christian Jews began to understand Jesus as the new Moses, as the sacrificial temple lamb, as King David's heir now ushering in God's kingdom.

Then, over ensuing centuries, Christians continued to see more in Jesus, relating him to their contemporary struggles, fears, and hopes. For example, by the fourth century, Jesus was understood as the victor over Satan, releasing the condemned from hell;[8] by the sixteenth-century Reformation, Jesus was seen as the all-sufficient atonement for sin, his "grace alone" being that which saves;[9] and by the twentieth century, with its emphasis on justice

---

8. This idea was first explored by the Early Church Father Origen, then further developed by Irenaeus, Athanasius, Chrysostom, and Augustine.

9. Martin Luther (1483–1546) made God's grace the revolutionary wind

and inclusion, Jesus has come to be seen as the embodiment of God's inclusive love and reconciling justice.[10]

Some theologians call this act of seeing more our *reconstructing* Jesus. But that word "reconstruction" is misleading if it makes it seem as though we're simply making things up about Jesus. I would say, instead, that the words and stories of Jesus keep revealing to us new depths. As I wrote earlier about The Sublime, The More isn't just a feature of external objects—it's something in us that is evoked by the object.

When I first moved to the Lake Tahoe area and consulted my maps, I only noticed the state highway that loops the lake. I had to live for months in Tahoe, to walk its trails and bike its paths, before I noticed all the other features that were, in fact, always on that map. I ignored them until real life pressed in upon me and opened my eyes.

That's what the stories of Jesus are like. Life presses in upon us—suffering, betrayal, religious hypocrisy, forgiveness, love, and new life from loss. Now we are prepared to see more in Jesus.

Here's what's most important for us. All these stories and claims about Jesus as "more" are used by his followers to say more not just about Jesus but about who we can be! This Jesus language circles back to us and spurs us to expand our humanity. Remember in chapter 1 how the phrase "God rested on the seventh day" boomerangs back to shape our action? It's the same thing here. So, language about Jesus boomerangs back to us. Jesus reveals "the more" of our humanity. He calls for more from us:

- more justice than we can imagine in our dealings with each other.
- more love than we are inclined to share.
- more truth than we are able or willing to see.

---

of the Reformation, followed by John Calvin (1509-1564) and Ulrich Zwingli (1484-1531).

10. Twentieth century liberation theologians, including Jürgen Moltmann, Gustavo Gutiérrez, James H. Cone, and Elizabeth Johnson, all emphasized God's inclusive community and justice in their work.

THE TRAIL OF REVERENCE BEFORE THE MORE

- more to life than the span between birth and death—resurrection.

Christians in every era have seen Jesus as a map for how to live. And there's more and more to that map.

THE MORE OF GOD

Just as Jesus reveals that we can be and do more, he also, in his teachings, invites us into a personal relationship with the source of his own "more"—God.

Jesus invites us to think of The More as a divine being who loves and cares for us—a "Father."[11] "Look at the birds of the air, for they neither sow nor reap nor gather into barns; yet your heavenly Father feeds them. Are you not of more value than they?" (Matt 6:26–34).

And so, in Jesus' teaching, The More is not just some amorphous something that surrounds our lives like a "blob of tapioca pudding," as C. S. Lewis once joked.[12] No! The More can be experienced as an abiding, eternal *personality*—that of a loving, providing parent who even cares for sparrows.

We might say that religious faith is living with confidence that our world is suffused with a loving personality, an infinite provider, a purposeful spirit who seeks our good—*God*.

What a wonder-filled, confident way to live. That's a map that gives courage!

REVERENCE WITHOUT RELIGION?

Yet, just like with the Sabbath discussed previously, you may not want to accept the religious dimensions of this experience: "Hey, can't I have my Sublime moments—without all this God stuff?" "Can't I have my 'more' without it being *The More*?"

---

11. See chapter 1, footnote 3 for a discussion about masculine language and images for God.

12. Lewis, *Miracles*, 117.

Just as before, you face a choice. Nonreligious hikers, divers, scientists, and philosophers do experience The More, The Sublime. But notice this: they may cut short, reduce, or block the mystery of The More. The nonbeliever may minimize her experience of awe, saying,

- "That mysterious 'more' is *nothing but* a lingering reaction from primitive days, when humans imagined gods behind the crack of thunder."
- "The Sublime is *nothing but* the pleasure of surviving an immense danger, like scaling a rocky peak."
- "Our experiences of transcendence are *nothing but* emotions soaring past the dictates of good sense and common reason."

These are all reductionist responses—reducing one's own exhilarating, expansive awareness to "This is nothing but . . ." Yet, remember what the great physicist Richard Feynman wrote? "Nothing is 'mere.' "

Yes, nothing is "mere"—there is More!

REVERENCE FOR THE MORE *OF LIFE:* YOUR RATIONAL DECISION

What will you choose? To live with the thrilling, spiritual meaning of your experiences of The Sublime—"I am part and parcel *of God*"?

Or to live in a paler, prosaic world of "This is nothing but . . ."?

Which map will guide you to deeper reverence before The More of life?

Chapter 3

The Trail of Revelation

WAITING FOR ANSWERS

They were stuck. The Kims' Saab station wagon couldn't move in the deep snow and ice of Bear Camp Road. Used to problem-solving in their professional lives, Kati and James were confident there was a solution. And for right now, things were okay. The car had gas enough to keep them warm through the night. As a lifelong camper, Kati had prepared the Saab with the basics of travel with kids, packing plenty of road food, cereal, and beverages, and she could breastfeed the baby.

But now, in the silence of that snowbound night, their senses went on high alert, searching for answers and assurance. That vague movement in the forest dark? Were they glimpsing a deer—or bear? That flutter in the outside breeze? Was that the beating of a search helicopter? Who might recognize they were missing, and when—the lodge, their friends, their house sitter, their colleagues?

The Kims were waiting for answers, scanning their environment, and searching their minds for answers that could save them. But the new morning brought no solutions. And the next day—and the next, and the next—brought neither answers nor rescue.

Snowbound since Sunday, November 26, by Saturday, December 2, they were desperate. They were forced, now, to create an answer.

Studying their paper map, they calculated that the little town of Galice was only four miles away. James would try to hike toward it and get help. And, if he couldn't make it, he promised Kati he'd return before the end of the day. [1]

NOT KNOWING AND REVELATION

The Kims were waiting for answers that exceeded what they could conceive or master for themselves. They were waiting for "revelation."

What is revelation? Revelation is that answer that emerges out of chaos, obstacles, and not knowing. These are, in fact, the very preconditions of revelation. There are some answers that can't be forced, or found in manuals or self-improvement apps. They seem to come from "beyond" ourselves.

This is what we call revelation.

Revelation isn't like incremental learning, some step-by-step process we manage. It is better described as "illumination." In revelation, *light* comes from beyond our own efforts and mastery. Revelation is less like a rational answer and more like an emotion-fueled submission to a greater reality. But before reality shines its light, first must come the storm.

---

1. Suh and Austin, "Kim."

The Trail of Revelation

LIFE NEEDS REVELATION

Why is revelation important? Life is but a series of obstacles, chaos, and times of not knowing, waiting, and scanning for answers—revelation. Life *is* Bear Camp Road!

Erik, you've an expert at facing the unknown, willingly choosing Bear Camp Road. You've learned to wait through uncertainty, trained by childhood's upheavals. I still have the photo of your first day of middle school: your swollen, red eyes from a sleepless night, and now morning tears. You did not want to leave the sweet, nurturing world of Oak Hills Elementary for the jungles of Meadow Park Middle School. Everything in you longed to go back—to stay where you felt known and valued.

That morning was so hard. And yet, you walked forward, through your fear. And now, twenty years later, you've lived in Nizhny Novgorod, in Chengdu, Shanghai, and Hong Kong. You've negotiated with a hostile landlord in Russian, charmed a girlfriend's parents in Cantonese, and spoken perfect Mandarin in high-risk job interviews.

But more, you've mastered the grammar of uncertainty. That language has expanded your life.

Indeed, no matter what our ages—twenty-somethings or sixty-plus—obstacles, not knowing, and chaos keep finding us. We must stand on Bear Camp Road.

RESISTANCE TO REVELATION

Yet not everyone experiences revelation. I've seen many older, supposedly wiser folks turn away from these preconditions necessary for revelation. They are not willing to sit with some chaos and live with uncertainty. They deny that they are confused and in conflict. They hold tight to tattered answers that no longer fit changing reality.

They call this "knowing what works."

Jesus likened these signs of resistance to trying to "pour new wine into old wineskins" (Luke 5:37). Chaos, uncertainty, and not knowing are like fermenting, volatile wine. Such young wine can't be poured into stiff, old wineskins. The old skins will eventually explode.

Contemporary scholars speak similarly. Historians of science talk about the way senior scientists resist new discoveries when emerging facts just won't fit into trusted, older paradigms.[2] Developmental psychologists document the disorientation experienced by those who can no longer "hold" new experiences within their old accommodating structures.[3] And master screenwriters know that every great story needs a "messy middle," where the hero must suffer and change.[4]

There's a famous film that illustrates this truth, and it's treasured by our family for that reason.

IT'S A WONDERFUL LIFE—AND REVELATION

You know how Dad always insists each Christmas season that we devote a night to watching *It's A Wonderful Life*? It's not just a Christmas tradition, however. This movie shows the life-and-death stakes for revelation.[5]

In this beloved movie, our hero, George Bailey, dreams he'll get out of small-town Bedford Falls and become an important man. He desires a life of travel and adventure, but he labors at the family business, The Bailey Brothers Building and Loan. Each evening he comes home to his old house, falling into disrepair. He's so frustrated and blue, that he can't pay attention to the antics of his charming children or the affections of his adoring wife, Mary.

---

2. Historians of science often cite Thomas Kuhn's important work, *The Structure of Scientific Revolutions*—itself a paradigm-shifting work.

3. See the widespread use of Jean Piaget's theory of assimilation and accommodation, based on his work, *Science of Education and the Psychology of the Child*.

4. Brené Brown adapted this lesson from screenwriters in her influential book *Rising Strong* (chs. 4 and 5), illustrating the essential stage of struggle that precedes illumination.

5. Capra, *It's a Wonderful Life*.

One night, in despair, George decides to throw himself off a bridge but is saved by an angel. The angel will grant George one special wish. George mutters in hopelessness, "I wish I had never been born." The angel takes this as George's actual wish and carries him on an invisible tour of his town and family, as though they existed without George's ever having lived.

Without George's leadership of The Building and Loan, his townspeople are exploited and impoverished by a ruthless businessman. Without George's love, the beautiful and vivacious Mary lives a lonely, anxious life, never marrying or having children. Without George's saving his kid brother from drowning in a frozen pond, his brother never goes on to save fellow soldiers in the war and win the Congressional Medal of Honor.

Seeing his world, absent his own existence, brings George's revelation. His aha moment allows him to see his life in a startling, new way. He now sees that his life is important and successful—but not in the terms he envisioned as a callow, impatient young man.

When authors or screenwriters plot out their story line, they intentionally create that aha moment, building the action and suspense toward it, and then showing how the key characters' lives are transformed by that revelation.

Can you see how crucial this aha moment is to George's very life? Without it, he would have died, throwing himself off a bridge. So, too, with us. Without our own moments of revelation, we can also "die"—we can grow stuck and embittered by the past, fail to advance in our work, shrink back from new experiences, and abandon relationships that would deepen our humanity.

MATURE FAITH

Waiting for answers demands what we can characterize as "mature faith." What does that mean?

- First, it is a faith that is *prepared* through study, service, and prayer. It is prepared to face and embrace the unknown. "By faith Noah, being warned by God concerning events as yet unseen, in reverent fear constructed an ark for the saving of his household" (Heb 11:7 ESV).

- Second, it is a faith that can *endure seasons of uncertainty*. We can "hold on" because we hold to a God we experience as good, one who works for our protection and provision. "'For I know the plans I have for you,' declares the Lord, 'plans to prosper you and not to harm you, plans to give you a hope and a future'" (Jer 29:11 NIV).

- Third, it is a faith that *opens our mind and heart* to answers from "beyond." Like the Kims on that first, frightening night, this faith is actively scanning. It actively watches for the Lord to open doors, especially unexpected ones. "But, as it is written, 'What no eye has seen, nor ear heard, nor the heart of man imagined, what God has prepared for those who love him'" (1 Cor 2:9 ESV).

YOUR RATIONAL DECISION ABOUT REVELATION

Can you wait patiently for revelation, for your crucial aha moments, without all this God stuff?

Yes, you can.

But religion teaches its followers to wait with endurance, expectation, even confidence. Through its stories and teachings, it repeatedly celebrates active and engaged waiting.

As one nineteenth-century preacher wrote, "This word, 'wait,' rightly describes almost the whole of Christian life, for waiting is active as well as passive, energetic as well as patient, and to wait upon the Lord necessitates . . . holy courage."[6]

That experience of waiting isn't just a bad patch to get through and survive. It's a season of deep, sustaining love, holding on to God in the wilderness.

Then comes revelation.

That leads us to our fourth trail—Resilience.

---

6. Spurgeon, "Brave Waiting."

CHAPTER *4*

The Trail of Resilience

KATI'S RESILIENCE

Thus far, we've looked at religion's maps for a life rhythm, reverence before The More of life, and revelation—the *aha moment*. Now we come to what many say is the most used map of religion: resilience. The maps of religion can show the way through suffering, injustice, defeat.

Psychologists say that resilience is the capacity to think clearly, to adapt, to not withdraw but seek out sources of love and strength. It includes the ability to shift perspective amid overwhelming obstacles.[1] Kati Kim showed all those features of resilience as she waited for James to reach Galice.

---

1. These features are often summarized in counseling and research literature as "The Four S's": Support, Strategy, Sagacity, Solution Seeking. See Riopel,

- Kati thought clearly. To keep up the family's strength, she carefully triaged their food supplies and harvested snow for drinking water.
- She adapted. Already nursing the baby, Kati decided to nurse the four-year-old to keep her nourished and comforted.
- She kept her emotional connection to others. Kati's love for her girls and James would not allow her to give up.
- She creatively shifted her perspective. Kati imagined what a search helicopter's perspective might be, hovering far above her. In preparation, she removed the car's vanity mirror to be ready as a reflective signal.[2]

TEENAGE RESILIENCE

Siri, I remember your resilience when we moved across the country to New Canaan, Connecticut, for my new job as a pastor. We found ourselves in an astonishingly affluent community where we were just "the church mice."

But you found a way forward. You adapted, drawing on familiar strengths from your old life. You connected with others, the girls' swim team, and found your new girl tribe. A reluctant hiker back in Oregon, you now shifted your perspective and became the outdoor expert for your new friends. You coped with the crisis of New Canaan's culture by becoming more yourself.

I remember Dad asking you one day, "Siri, who are the cool kids at high school?" You smiled and said, "*I am*, Dad! I am the cool kid from Oregon!"

RELIGIOUS RESILIENCE: THE MENNONITE HOSTAGES

Here's another story of resilience, where religious faith makes all the difference.

"Resilience Examples."
   2. Roberts, "Kati Kim."

The Trail of Resilience

Mennonite missionaries had sustained a decades-long ministry of service in Haiti, despite natural disasters, civic breakdown, and violence. The Mennonites built and repaired homes and schools. They assisted the most vulnerable, including widows and the handicapped, training them as teachers, nurses, carpenters, and helpers—an investment in Haiti's resilience.

And then the Mennonites' own resilience faced the ultimate test: they were taken hostage by an outlaw gang in the autumn of 2021.

> As they became aware of what was happening at the time of capture, the group began singing the chorus, "The angel of the Lord encampeth round about them that fear Him, and delivereth them," based on Psalm 34:7. This song became a favorite of theirs, and they sang it many times throughout their days of captivity. The hostages . . . spent many hours of each day praying, singing, and encouraging each other. . . . They did not have a Bible, but they recited Bible verses by memory among themselves. They prayed for their captors and told them about God's love and their need to repent.[3]

Could you endure a situation like that—without some kind of faith? Could you endure the threat of death, relying on your own self-confidence? Could you sustain yourself with the bromides of secular culture—"Manifest what you want into existence" (New Age bestseller *The Law of Attraction*); "No one is coming. It's up to you" (podcaster Mel Robbins); "If you can't, you must. If you must, you can" (motivational speaker Tony Robbins).[4]

Perhaps.

But religious faith frees us to endure and act, confident of our connection to a higher power that sustains us, second by second. With faith, we are not alone in such trials! That divine connection provides a home of sustaining love and strength. That connection becomes a safe dwelling place where the angel of the Lord encampeth near.

3. Troyer, "Hostages Freed."
4. Robbins, "No One Is Coming"; Robbins, "20 Best."

Eight Trails

HOW FAITH HOLDS US

How does religious faith, seen in those Mennonite hostages, provide resilience? Does such faith demand there's some divine superman who swoops in and saves the day?

No. Once again, we'll look at human behavior for the lived meaning of religious beliefs. As we've said in earlier chapters, beliefs about God show their meaning by how they get used. And we've seen already that these beliefs "boomerang" back to us, shaping our behavior.

So, how does belief in God shape resilience? Belief in a loving, protecting God provides what psychologists call a "holding environment." A pioneering scholar of human development, D. W. Winnicott used "holding environment" to describe the psychological space one experiences when one feels safe—especially safe enough to explore and risk.[5] "Holding" is provided through the care of an abiding, loving person who does not overprotect and smother.

In infancy, one's first holding environment is provided, typically, by one's parents. Each stage of our developmental journey and life's work, ideally, provides us with other such holding environments.

Faith in God, then, is a *divine* holding environment where the believer feels that he is safe, but also that he's enabled to strike out into the unknown and take a risk, confident he'll be "held." That sense of being held by God extends even to danger and death.

Thus, people of faith can experience an unshakable safety. William James's masterpiece on religious psychology, *The Varieties of Religious Experience*, repeatedly describes the unusual sense of safety known by committed believers.[6] James describes it (with

---

5. Winnicott, "Parent-Infant Relationship."

6. James concludes with a summary of the characteristics found in ordinary believers, especially emphasizing safety: "An assurance of safety and a temper of peace . . ." James, *Varieties*, 61. This emphasis on safety arises from many interviews by James and others, such as this from a forty-nine-year-old man: "God is more real to me than any thought or thing or person. . . . He answers me again and again, often in words so clearly spoken . . . usually a text

some bafflement): "If you ask how religion thus falls on the thorns and faces death, and in the very act annuls annihilation, I cannot explain the matter, for it is religion's secret, and to understand it you must yourself have been a religious man."[7]

As those Mennonites repeatedly sang in their hymn, "So, when death's hour draws nigh, I need not fear; / The angel of Thy love will still be near."[8]

DEATH AND RESILIENCE

Especially as we face our own mortality or lose a beloved through death, we need resilience. Here, religious people have tested maps of guidance. They have sacred scriptures, familiar rituals, beloved music, and ancient teachings that help them through this wilderness.

Admittedly, the world's great religions have quite different ideas about what happens when we die. Is "that place" a realm of joyful reunion with loved ones (popular "heaven" books), a resurrection into a radically different sort of body (traditional Christianity), reincarnation into another life (Hinduism), dissolution of our impermanent self into not-self (Buddhism)? (I'll have more to say about an afterlife in the final, eighth trail: "Resurrection.")

But, as we have been saying throughout this book, we're going to turn our attention to *this* world—to human behavior we can observe, not invisible divine beings. So, what *do* the religious do with their beliefs?

Let's look at those Mennonites. Their traditional beliefs about Christ and God's power shaped their response to their captivity—those beliefs boomeranged back to their own lives. So, just as Jesus commanded and did himself, they prayed for their "enemies," their captors—probably within earshot of them! They daily reminded these violent gang members that they loved them and forgave

---

of Scripture, unfolding some new view of him and his love for me, and care for my safety." James, *Varieties*, 318.

7. James, *Varieties*, 48.
8. Hawks, "Angel of the Lord," verse 3.

them—just like Jesus Christ. And they unceasingly prayed for their own release. They waited expectantly, preparing themselves, confident God's power could open doors.

When that open door finally appeared after two anxious months of captivity, they were ready. They quietly escaped into the night, walking for miles over difficult terrain, guided by the stars.[9]

STOICISM AND RESILIENCE

Resilience is an essential skill for any life. And, in these past few years, we've all been enrolled in a master class on resilience, brought on by the pandemic and its continuing impact on health, finances, and politics.

Many have chosen to be tutored by the ancient Stoics for this master class. As I began to draft this chapter in the later days of the pandemic, there were already fourteen books about Stoicism on Amazon's website. Today, in mid-2025, thousands of titles are listed. And books alone won't slake our Stoic thirst: Stoic-focused websites are multiplying, and there is a whole new marketplace of Stoic mugs, pendants, and quote-a-day calendars!

Why this hunger for a philosophy that originated around 300 BC? Because Stoicism focuses on resilience. This ancient philosophy, now popularized for a contemporary, American audience, incorporates key teachings about how to be resilient.

For example, Stoics train their minds to "reframe"—as modern psychology would put it. One ancient training exercise, called "the view from above," has us picture ourselves as part of a larger cosmos and human community. Another Stoic exercise, the "daily review," has us reflect on the day's events and our responses, seeking improvement. A modern Stoic exercise, proposed by popular Stoic interpreter David Fideler, has us imagine that a wise person (like Socrates) is watching over our actions so that we act in accordance with that person's spirit and teaching.[10]

---

9. Smith, "Church Agency."
10. Fideler, *Breakfast with Seneca*, 218.

THE TRAIL OF RESILIENCE

Is there something familiar in all this?

Does the "view from above" remind you of Christianity's "communion of the saints"—a cosmic community of souls that transcends time and space?

Does the "daily review" remind you of traditional daily prayers, where believers examine their actions and motives (like the popular Jesuit *Examen* prayer)?

Does Fideler's exercise in imagining Socrates also remind you of "WWJD"—"What would Jesus do?"

Well then, let's ask: Is Stoicism a *religion*?

RELIGION, OR SIMPLY WATERED-DOWN ADVICE?

Stoicism's attraction for many moderns is its promise of religion's benefits *without* religion, as noted by this observer: "Some contemporary proponents of Stoicism . . . present it as a strategy for living a meaningful secular existence, as though Stoicism might be swapped in for religion like Lactaid for regular milk. (Got a God intolerance? Try Epictetus!)"[11]

But, on closer inspection, genuine Stoicism seems more akin to religion. It emphasizes strength derived from beyond one's powers. It promotes mystical wisdom that demands a humble openness. It promotes living aligned with Ultimate Reality. And that Ultimate Reality isn't some mute, molecular material. No, it's alive with Being, in which we all participate, called by Stoics "the Logos."[12] (Of course, *that* term reminds us of the Christian Scripture, "In the Beginning, was theWord" [John 1:1]—the *Logos*.)

In the words of best-selling Stoic interpreter David Fideler,

> The world for [the Stoics] was alive, numinous, and sacred—animated by a living spirit. And they were part of that world. Every part of creation spoke to them—brooks, trees, and mountains—and they responded appropriately with myth, story, and song, in a vital spirit of participation. . . . The ancient Greeks saw life and divinity

11. Young, "Better Living."
12. Fideler, *Breakfast with Seneca*, 60.

in all things. Deeply moved by the order and beauty of nature, the ancient thinkers set out on a quest to understand the cosmic pattern and our own relation to it . . . the cosmos as a living organism with which we are bound in vital participation.[13]

So, what does this mean for us? Just this: many secular philosophies of resilience—including modern Stoicism—draw deeply from religion's wells. It is as though, to adapt a phrase from one critic, religion has been "spilt" into these secular solutions.[14] This "spilt" religion is not the same as the articulated beliefs and organized training provided by the world's great faiths. Nonetheless, religion is *spilling* into these modern, secular forms, a wellspring for their philosophies.

The question, then, for us is this: Are secular philosophies, based on "spilt" religion, simply "watered-down" advice?

Perhaps secular philosophies can help us in our day-to-day frustrations and trials. But when an existential crisis hits, will we find ourselves crying out, "Oh God, help me, help me"?

YOUR RATIONAL DECISION ABOUT RESILIENCE

Can you count on and experience resilience in the darkest moments of life "without all this God stuff"?

Perhaps.

You can try. You can try to "manifest what you want into existence." You can lean on family, friends, political groups, or even a supportive church.

But they themselves may falter, be frail, be too human, and disappoint.

They may not have the full measure of wisdom, constancy, or strength you'll need.

They may even betray you.

---

13. Fideler, *Breakfast with Seneca*, 218.
14. Hulme, "Romanticism and Classicism."

THE TRAIL OF RESILIENCE

They may not be willing or even able to walk with you through the wilderness.

But the relationship with God will not fail when all the others crumble. Feeling held and safe, and thus inspired to risk, a relationship with God gives resilience.

That leads us to our fifth trail—the Trail of Relationship.

Chapter 5

The Trail of Relationship

KATI'S RELATIONSHIPS

As her little girls gazed into her face, Kati Kim knew her fears could not betray their trust. And she felt James's spirit was with her. Although he was physically far off, making his way for help, his strength and love enveloped and empowered her.

Beyond this intimate family of four, Kati thought about her other relationships. She was confident her large circle of family and friends was working tirelessly to find them.

In those horrible days of uncertain survival, Kati imagined and meditated on all the faces she loved and trusted. She had a map for those days of frightening uncertainty: relationships of love. That map kept her centered and courageous.

The Trail of Relationship

WE'RE WIRED FOR RELATIONSHIP

Human life is impossible without such maps of relationship. We're lost and wither without the assurance of someone who truly cares, someone whose face we can see or imagine.

In the 1980s there was a surge of abandoned babies in Romania; they were placed in orphanages but essentially warehoused, left alone in their cribs except for impersonal diaper changes and feedings. Without the loving touch of a consistent caregiver, tens of thousands of children were permanently damaged, emotionally and physically. A famous study of those children found that about 40 percent of the teens who had grown up in the orphanages had a major psychiatric condition.[1] Many experienced stunted physical growth, and their motor skills and language development stalled. If you think of the brain as a light bulb, it's as though they had a dimmer. "Instead of a 100-watt light bulb, it was a 40-watt light bulb," said Harvard professor Charles Nelson, a leader of the study.[2]

Our need for relationship begins at birth, impacting our fundamental biology. But we never outgrow that need to be embraced, consoled, and enjoyed. A primal sense of connection characterizes the most advanced adult development. Thriving marriages, effective workplace teams, wise governments, and compelling service organizations are characterized by a deep sense of shared connection and duty to each other.

---

1. Humphreys et al., "Effects of Institutional Rearing." Launched in 2000, the Bucharest Early Intervention Project was a rigorously controlled investigation that included 136 abandoned infants and toddlers. The children were randomly assigned either to remain in orphanage care or be placed in family foster care. The study found that those who remained in orphanages were severely impaired in IQ and manifested a variety of social and emotional disorders, as well as changes in brain development. Those in foster care showed improvements, especially relative to how young they were at the time of foster placement.

2. Nelson, as quoted in Hamilton, "Orphans' Lonely Beginnings."

Eight Trails

ALL YOU NEED ARE FRIENDS?

Young adults especially need relationships with older adults to navigate life's roads. Parents and peers just aren't enough. Young adults navigating life's uncertainties need caring adults who can offer career advice and networking, a steady presence when times get rocky, and can model happy, mature lifestyles.

In a new study of working-class young adults who managed to beat the odds and graduate from college, almost all had significant relationships with caring adults, especially finding them in their churches. The author writes,

> Teenage boys from working-class families, regardless of race, who were regularly involved in their church and strongly believed in God were twice as likely to earn bachelor's degrees as moderately religious or nonreligious boys. Religious boys are not any smarter, so why are they doing better in school? . . . Why does religion give . . . an academic advantage? *Because it offers them the social capital that affluent teenagers can get elsewhere.* Religious communities keep families rooted to a place and help kids develop trusting relationships with youth ministers and friends' parents who share a common outlook on life. Collectively, these adults encourage teenagers to follow the rules and avoid antisocial behaviors.[3]

Conversely, working-class young adults will struggle when they are unanchored to a network of adults who counsel and advocate for them. They can become unfocused and unemployed, unconnected to a supportive community and a cause that inspires perseverance. They are vulnerable to "Deaths of Despair," including drug overdoses and alcohol-related injuries and illness.[4]

Does a higher income insulate young adults from these obstacles? Yes, to some extent. Higher-income parents accrue "social

---

3. Horwitz, "I Followed the Lives"; emphasis added.

4. This phrase was coined by Nobel Prize winner Angus Deaton and fellow economist Anne Case in their groundbreaking account of the deadly consequences of the weakening power of labor, job flight from rural America, and unaffordable health care. Case and Deaton, *Deaths of Despair*.

capital" they can use for their children's advantage: these parents network with colleagues for their kids' job interviews, advice, and references; they polish their children's social skills through memberships in private clubs; and they even teach them athletic skills that can position their children professionally, like tennis, golf, and skiing.

But ultimately, every real relationship—whether one is rich or not—gets tested.

ROCKY ROAD AHEAD!

No one is immune from the breakdown of relationships that inform our identity. Conflict erupts at work among long-standing colleagues or business partners; a marriage becomes strained by life's normal challenges; children's misbehavior drives parents to mistrust their kids and withhold rewards; longtime friends feel betrayed when they disagree on controversial issues.

How does the secular world help in these difficult passages? In a word, *problematize.*

The secular world problematizes these conflicts as aberrations of the "norm." They see relationship upheaval as abnormal, toxic, and violations of "what you deserve." They are sometimes seen as evidence of mental illness—and, of course, it's "the other person" who's ill.

Religion's approach is different. In contrast, religion normalizes relationship stress as part of the human condition. It teaches its followers that humans are prone to selfishness and self-illusion—what Christianity calls "fallen" or "sinful." Religion's sacred stories illustrate human families and marriages riddled with anger, envy, disappointment, and betrayal.

These stories teach that you cannot expect perfect relationships with mere mortals—and, by the way, you're the most mortal of all!

Eight Trails

HOW THE RELIGIOUS DO RELATIONSHIP: SOME RESEARCH

Yet, despite religion's teaching about human selfishness and sin, its followers also insist that there is sacred value and even a divine design in family and marriage relationships.

The authors of one study found that religious practices (such as forgiveness) help at every stage of conflict. They help, first, to prevent conflict. Then, these practices are a guide amidst conflict. Finally, these practices bring resolution to conflict.

Here are some quotes by those interviewed in the study:

> One of the basic teachings of the Savior is forgiveness so . . . if you want to be forgiven, the Bible teaches that you need to forgive other people. And, obviously we're imperfect and we want to be forgiven, and so I think both of us bring that idea or principle into our marriage relationship, and we see that we have to be willing to forgive the other person and . . . that influences our ability to maybe forgive a little bit sooner than we normally would have because we know and believe that forgiving is a good thing, something you should do.

> And, so it's a commitment to, to a way of life. It's a commitment to, not just for the here and now, it's a commitment to make things work and not just throw our hands up in the air and say, "Well I'm not in love with you anymore; [or] if you can't agree with that, let's just bag this whole thing."

> Well, I think the one thing that we've decided is that marriage is forever and no one's leaving so, you're going to have to work this out. We're going to have to come to some agreement because no one's going anywhere.

> There's no option to be angry or bitter at each other. It forces you to work.

The Trail of Relationship

> We go to church in the car every Sunday. We each ask individually; each member asks every other member of the family individually for forgiveness.[5]

Religion provides a unique and profound map that's been tested over countless miles of marriage and family conflicts. Religious practices and communities show their members how to face the challenges of love and daily life, and navigate toward peace. Indeed, in almost every measure of marriage and family well-being,[6] those who are active in their faith score higher than those with no religious practice in these categories: marriage happiness, keeping the family unit together, fulfillment at work, lower incidences of children's learning challenges, lower rates of abuse of alcohol and drugs—even significantly higher levels of sexual satisfaction with one's spouse![7]

I AND THOU

We've been focused on the stresses of human relationships, but let's return to their strengths. As noted in our opening section, we need to be embraced, enjoyed, and feel connected to others for our well-being.

In short, we need to be seen—literally seen and spiritually seen. We need face-to-face relationships where we dwell in mutual presence, listening, and understanding. We need "I and Thou" relationships.

The twentieth-century Jewish philosopher, rabbi, and mystic Martin Buber first used that term "I and Thou" in his book of the same name.[8]

---

5. All quotes taken from Lambert and Dollahite, "How Religiosity Helps," 445; brackets and ellipses original to source.

6. See Marri, "Marriage and Family" for extensive reports.

7. See Fagan and Nagai, "Marital Happiness"; "Divorce"; "Work Fulfillment"; "Children"; "Drinks Too Much"; "Feels Thrilled"; and Fagan, "Adolescent Hard Drug Use."

8. Buber, *I and Thou*.

That phrase describes relationships where two people are fully present to one another, in openhearted awareness and care, without any agenda or judgment. The I and Thou relationship helps us grow our inner life, authentic identity, and worth.

Yet however profound, the most ordinary human relationships can be such I and Thou relationships. As infants, we experienced the loving gaze of a parent, who delighted in our growth. In friendships, we experience the intimacy of sharing fun, secrets, and fears. In a romantic partner, we find that special someone who cherishes us, body and soul. These everyday relationships, in their very best moments, are I and Thou relationships.

THE EVOLVING I

As a parent, I learned the profound responsibility and joy of being a "Thou" to my children. Erik and Siri, from the earliest days, I tried to offer you my full attention, my loving gaze, my patient presence. In those moments, I was not just parenting you. You were *evolving* through the power of my "I."

But now, something tender and astonishing has happened in this season of life. John and I are evolving through the power of your "I."

In our older years, your loving presence is changing us. You text us and call us constantly—not from obligation but from relationship. It often feels like we're hanging out together, sharing a leisurely weekend breakfast. You ask us how we're doing in our new town: Are we making friends? Have we found new places to take the bikes? Do we have a tennis group yet?

You are evolving who we are becoming in our sixties and seventies. We would not be the people we are now without the "Thou" of our children.

The Trail of Relationship

RELATIONSHIP WITH GOD

I and Thou relationships are, at their heart, spiritual. Why "spiritual"?

Because the I and Thou encounter has an invisible quality, a *something* that can't be objectified or analyzed. Yet this encounter is the most real and important "thing" in our lives and affects us most profoundly.

A relationship with God is just like that! God, by any definition of god, cannot be objectified, described, or analyzed. Yet, despite this "nonobjective" status, God is the most important thing in the lives of believers and affects them most profoundly.[9] God is never an "it" to a believer, yet is absolutely real. God can't be described, yet through this relationship, we learn who we really are and can more clearly describe ourselves.

Buber emphasized that all our I and Thou relationships—with others, with nature, with our beloved pets—prepare us for God's I and Thou. But God is a special "Thou" in this regard: of all those other Thou's, God sees us most completely. He sees our strengths, our secrets, our sins. He understands where we've come from, how we've struggled, and where we could progress.

His own unlimited, eternal spirit beholds us fully, as only a heavenly "father" could. As the Christian apostle Paul wrote, "When we cry, 'Abba! Father!' it is that very Spirit bearing witness with our spirit that we are children of God" (Rom 8:15–16).

This is Spirit meeting our spirit.

In God's gaze, we are truly seen and most fully ourselves. The divine Thou brings so much more to the I and Thou than any mere human could. Yet, this divine relationship does not diminish but enriches our other relationships. Because of our relationship with God, we now better know ourselves and bring that wisdom to others.

---

9. As Buber describes it, "I can neither experience nor describe the form which meets me, but only body it forth.... If test is made of its objectivity, the form is certainly not 'there.' Yet what is actually so much present as it is? And the relation in which I stand to it is real, for it affects me, as I affect it." Buber, *I and Thou*, 10.

Eight Trails

YOUR RATIONAL DECISION ABOUT RELATIONSHIPS AND FAITH

We've considered two very different reasons for a religious map for relationships.

The first was pragmatic. Objective, peer-reviewed research proves that religious faith and practice help sustain marriages and families. Those studies can be supplemented by your own observations. Ask a religious person how they use faith in their relationships. You may be surprised that faith makes them especially thoughtful and intentional about relationships—not robotic rule followers who fear authority figures. Their attitude toward a spouse or parent is not blind obedience and fear but mindfulness and resolve, guided by their faith.

The second reason was spiritual. Our most important relationships—I and Thou relationships—are spiritual. An I and Thou relationship with God is the most expansive and empowering of these I and Thou's. In God's presence, you'll experience yourself as completely known and cherished. In God's gaze, you can face yourself with all your problems and potential, and experience God's grace. Released from the burdens of your past, you'll hear Thou calling you forward.

In response to your honest question, "Can't I have a good marriage and family, without all this God stuff?" the research shows you're taking your chances. "Can't I have meaningful friendships without a relationship with God?" Yes, but in the gaze of God's Thou you'll discover who you really are and bring that wisdom to your friendships.

THE WAY AHEAD

Religions are committed to binding together families for the sake of something greater—serving God's design for their family *and* their world. Indeed, the original meaning of religion is from the Latin "bind together."[10]

---

10. See the etymology for this word at *Oxford English Dictionary*, s.v.

THE TRAIL OF RELATIONSHIP

There is one more way religion can be a powerful force for binding together. It can bind us to divine strength and wisdom to withstand destructive human impulses.

That takes us to our sixth trail—Regulating our impulses.

"religion," last updated 2009, https://www.oed.com/dictionary/religion_n?tab=factsheet.

Chapter 6

The Trail of Regulation

KATI'S HUNGER

Kati Kim had packed food for their holiday road trip: snack bars, fruit, chips, and drinks. That food would have been a delicious distraction on the long trip—not really needed for hunger. But now, on Bear Camp Road, those treats became key to survival.

As Kati wrote months later, "As a mother of two small children and lifelong camper, I tend to be over-prepared. We were also on a 9-day road trip, so we had a decent amount of supplies. We'd packed everything from foods & beverages (nonperishable food, bottled beverages).... We never once ran out of food & did have access to clean water (when fresh water became scarce, we used large empty bottles for melting snow in the sun, or in the car with

THE TRAIL OF REGULATION

body heat). Once it was clear we were stranded, it was my job to ration the food."[1]

Kati had to eat with the utmost care. Her priority was the children's survival, so eating had one focus—to sustain her nursing milk supply, which was now the children's main nourishment.

She had to regulate her hunger and the human pleasure of eating.

ERIK'S CHRISTMAS REGULATION

And sometimes, it's a child who understands this best.

I'll never forget one Christmas morning, watching Erik demonstrate stunning self-regulation as a grade-schooler. While the rest of us tore into our presents in a frenzy of fun and desire, Erik calmly lined up his gifts and declared he would open just one a day. With skeptical admiration, we watched him over the coming days, savoring each present, prolonging his joy. The following year, remembering his ritual of restraint, I made sure he had twelve gifts under the tree, to celebrate the twelve days of Christmas. What began as a simple act of self-control became a cherished tradition.

WE'RE ALREADY SELF-REGULATING

In both challenging and daily situations, we recognize that those who can regulate their hunger—for not just food but for security, power, sex, and pleasure—can live better lives.

We naturally seek out self-regulation
- over our destructive thoughts and self-sabotaging ways, so some engage in counseling or self-help groups;
- over unhealthy eating, so some adopt restrictive diets, from online calorie counters to bariatric surgery;
- over stress and distracted thinking, so many practice daily meditation and even join meditation retreats;

---

1. Rede, "Kati Kim Speaks Out."

- over our sleeping, our steps, our moods, so many now use "wearables";
- over excessive self-absorption from all of the above, so we decide to "think like a monk," just like Jay Shetty's book by the same name.

Yet, when it comes to religion, *its* rules and regulations seem the very reason many people reject religion. "The church is always judging people and trying to control them!" "The church is led by hypocrites who do what they preach against!" "The church judges others who sin—that is, those who sin differently than they do!"

But when you think of it, *everyone* has a stake in the regulation of desire. This isn't just a matter of personal lifestyle or self-development—our desires, left unchecked, can destroy families and damage society. According to a 1994 psychological work, "Self-regulation failure is the major social pathology of the present time."[2] The writers go on to describe how failures in human self-control are at fault for most of modern society's ills: unregulated sexual activity leads to fatherless children, undisciplined spending leads to debt's despair, unstructured eating leads to obesity and its related diseases, undemanding schooling leads to youths unable to learn and adapt to a volatile labor market.[3]

And our planet has a stake in the regulation of desire. Unless we can curb our hunger for fossil fuel energy and unbounded consumption, our planet will be in peril. Unregulated human desire is, in fact, the cause of global warming.

Do I have your attention yet? Human self-regulation can be pursued for the sake of self-improvement. But society's good and the planet's survival especially depend on our self-regulation.

THE ABUSE OF RELIGIOUS REGULATION

We agree that the regulation of desire is a necessary habit for everyone's good.

2. Baumeister et al., *Losing Control*, 3.
3. Baumeister et al., *Losing Control*.

The Trail of Regulation

But now, let's face what's on your mind with your protests against religious regulations. It's sex, I know.

You're right that religion has regulated sexuality with condemning judgments and discriminatory laws. Religion has denounced homosexuals and those with nonconforming gender identities, ostracized them from their community, and driven them into secret lives. Many religions continue to prohibit divorce, despite spousal cruelty and abandonment. And these regulations and their abusive impact have been justified by scripture.

Scripture, as well, is the source of another common form of abuse—the abuse of children in the name of God. The Hebrew book of Proverbs counsels, "Do not withhold discipline from a child; though you strike him with the rod, he will not die" (Prov 23:13 NASB).

And let's not forget that nugget from Deuteronomy that advises parents of incorrigible sons to let the city's elders stone their sons to death.[4]

Here's a small but stunning example from American history. In 1831 Francis Wayland, a Baptist minister and the fourth president of Brown University, decided one day that he had to break the *stubborn will of his fifteen-month-old infant.* He isolated the toddler in his bedroom and withheld bread and milk until the toddler finally came to him and asked him "sweetly" for food. This so-called fast lasted from Thursday at five o'clock in the evening until Saturday at three o'clock in the afternoon! And Reverend Wayland was so impressed by his program of regulation that he described it in an essay for his fellow Baptists.[5]

---

4. "If any man has a stubborn and rebellious son who will not obey his father or his mother, and when they chastise him, he will not even listen to them, then his father and mother shall seize him, and bring him out to the elders of his city at the gateway of his hometown. And they shall say to the elders of his city, 'This son of ours is stubborn and rebellious, he will not obey us, he is a glutton and a drunkard.' Then all the men of his city shall stone him to death; so you shall remove the evil from your midst, and all Israel shall hear of it and fear" (Deut 21:18–21 NASB).

5. Wayland, "Case of Conviction."

Yes, it's an ugly part of religion. The regulation of human desire can tip into discrimination, violence, broken lives, and abuse.

THE POSITIVE POWER OF RELIGIOUS REGULATION: SUPER-REGULATORS

Is there anything positive to say about religion's regulation of desire? The therapies, wearables, and bariatric surgeries of the secular world seem, by comparison, awfully tame!

The power—and, yes, the danger—of religious regulation is that it springs from community aspiration, supported by ancient teachings and the felt power of God's will. And religious communities celebrate those who excel in such regulation, whom we might call "super self-regulators."

Those super-regulators are an important class of people that we see across religions—they're typically called "ascetics." Ascetics practice self-discipline and renunciation of worldly pleasures to draw closer to the divine. But that experience of closeness with divine power often leads them back to serve their communities. Their self-regulating behavior benefits their community, not just themselves.

For example, Buddhism teaches detachment from pleasures, possessions, and human relationships in the quest for enlightenment. It would seem that the "higher" one goes in Buddhism, the more one would withdraw from others. Yet those most advanced in this quest for enlightenment choose to "return" to the realm of relationships and worldly concerns, in an act of extraordinary compassion for others. These super self-regulators are called "bodhisattvas," and they take this vow: "Any may come and ask, and I shall give as they desire to have."[6]

Hinduism, Islam, and Christianity have their own versions of such ascetic practices and holy people, practicing self-regulation not just for self-advancement but for the sake of others. These super self-regulators wield unusual influence in their communities

---

6. Chödrön, *No Time to Lose*, 19, 66–68.

but eschew the entrapments of worldly power. We think of ascetics such as Dorothy Day, Mahatma Gandhi, Simone Weil, Thích Nhất Hạnh, and Mother Teresa who regarded their fame with ambivalence but deployed it strategically for others' good.

I think especially of John Muir, whose forest trails you're now discovering in your trips to Yosemite, Mammoth, and other national parks. Muir explored the Sierras and American West with just a loaf of bread and some tea. A devout Christian, he explained his diet as "feeding on God's abounding, inexhaustible spiritual beauty bread."[7] Influenced by his readings of the Gospels, Muir had no taste for property or power. Yet, for the sake of saving Yosemite from developers and ranchers, he entered the realm of politics, lobbying leaders and writing articles and letters.

Muir even escorted Teddy Roosevelt into Yosemite, where the two outdoorsmen declined the tents used by Roosevelt's party, choosing to sleep under the late autumn stars. They awakened in the morning, covered by snow![8]

THE CONNECTED CONSCIOUSNESS OF SELF-REGULATORS

What characterizes the consciousness of these super self-regulators, such as John Muir, Dorothy Day, Gandhi, and Mother Teresa?

These extraordinary people experience a continuity of life with God that extends to God's creation. You might say that the internal map of their being includes God and all creation. Although their lives are very different from most others, they do not experience themselves as alien from others, but as deeply felt companions.

William James described the saintly, ascetic character in these terms:

1. "A feeling of being in a wider life than that of this world's selfish little interests."

---

7. Huber, "John Muir's Menu."
8. King, *Guardians*, xxxii.

2. "A sense of the friendly continuity of the ideal power [God] with our own life, and a willing self-surrender to its control."
3. "An immense elation and freedom, as the outlines of the confining selfhood melt down."
4. "A shifting of the emotional center towards loving and harmonious affections, towards 'yes, yes,' and away from 'no,' where the claims of the non-ego are concerned."[9]

Just as Katie Kim, so continuous with her daughters' lives that she can curb her hunger for their sake, so the ascetic feels so continuous with God's life that he can curb his various hungers to serve God and others.

WHAT DOES RELIGION ADD TO REGULATION?

But nonbelievers can affirm and follow these same practices, right? You don't have to believe in God to control yourself and serve others, as many nonbelievers insist. You can curb your destructive impulses, you can commit to nonviolent activism, you can face and change the bigotry of your culture—all without belief in a higher power.

What does religious belief add to regulating behavior? Well, religion offers a developmental path from subtle, social coercion to freely chosen self-discipline. Regulation may begin with the rules a religious culture imposes on its novice believers, but it can culminate in mature *self*-discipline. The believer *desires* these good behaviors and can hardly act otherwise.

To an outside observer, religion may seem to be obsessed with regulation—"repression," nonbelievers may call it. But believers experience their faith as redirecting their desires toward a higher pleasure.[10] They desire to serve the Lord; they desire to attain an inner peace; they desire to embody the best of their religion's ideals; they desire to win eternal life. These desires come to override

---

9. James, Varieties, 186–187.
10. Smith, *You Are What You Love.*

more transient desires to self-indulge, to lash out in anger, to live for this hour, to fit in with the crowd.

How does religious faith further this redirection and refinement of our desires? Not so much through didactic teaching and authoritarian demands, but through compelling emotions, experiences, and relationships. As James K. A. Smith writes in his much-awarded book, *You Are What You Love*, religion saturates its believers with alternative pleasures—a beautiful life not through consumerism but through community service; worship that satisfies rather than entertainment that leaves us empty; friendships based on spiritual values rather than financial success. Our desires are redirected and refined toward pleasures that are lasting, other-focused, and truly free.

The only question then is, "Are we free to turn toward these higher pleasures, or are we imprisoned, unable to change?"

And here religion offers that "higher power" which enables us to change. Christians call it "grace"—an unearned and effortless strength that comes from beyond—from the Lord. It enables us to slowly—or even instantaneously for some—change destructive habits and climb toward self-control, freely chosen.

Yes, I know you can be good without God. But a deeper, sustained, more selfless goodness is possible *with* God. A religious community and its practices not only regulate our behavior, they can set us on a path to freely chosen self-control.

A key step on that path is facing ourselves—our stumbling, our intentional and unintentional wrongdoing, our complicity in evil. That brings us to the seventh trail—Repentance.

CHAPTER 7

The Trail of Repentance

MISSED DAYS AND MISTAKES

Those dedicated to rescuing the Kims lost precious hours and days.

On Tuesday, November 28, some friends noticed the family missing from commitments they had planned. On Wednesday, November 29, the house sitter reported them missing to the local police, but the officer in charge of missing persons was out sick. The official search would not begin until Thursday, November 30.

On Friday, December 1, two cell phone engineers heard the story of the missing family and wondered if they could help by tracking the Kims' cell phone transmissions. Offering their expertise to the official search team, inexplicably, they were rebuffed.

They were determined to continue but then encountered privacy rules that stalled them for another day.

On Saturday, December 2, they detected that the Kims' phone had connected with a cell tower near Glendale, Oregon, on Sunday, November 26, around one-thirty in the morning. They then used a computer program to triangulate an area accessible to that tower: it was the Bear Camp area. They called the Medford police immediately—at six o'clock in the evening on December 2. They pleaded with the police to relay their findings to the search team.[1]

Meanwhile, that very afternoon a Medford man was driving with his wife to cut a Christmas tree. As John Rachor drove, his wife read aloud the story of the missing Kim family, just published in the local paper. Immediately, Rachor wanted to join the search for the Kims. But family plans delayed his resolve.

The next day, however, Rachor did join the search—Sunday, December 3. An experienced amateur helicopter pilot, he knew the area intimately and had an intuition about Bear Camp Road. He flew over the Bear Camp area and noticed tire tracks in the snow. But his fuel was running low, so he had to turn back.

Alarmed over what he'd seen, Rachor returned early Monday morning. Now he saw that the snowy tire tracks showed that no vehicle had driven back out—just two clear lines of tracks, no turnaround. Then he recognized human footprints! Immediately, he radioed the other searchers. Rachor had to turn back to refuel but quickly returned. Flying overhead, his heart leaped as he spotted Mrs. Kim with her daughters, near the road. He radioed the family's position to the authorities, and within an hour they were rescued![2]

But the rescuers' excitement turned to despair as Kati told them that James had left that Saturday—three days earlier—to try to get to Galice.

The searchers finally discovered James's body sixteen miles away, face down by a creek. It was Wednesday, December 5.

1. Suo and Suh, "Kim Case."
2. Lednicer, "Following a Hunch."

Eight Trails

REGRET—OR REPENT?

Those searching for the Kim family were left with regrets, questions, and sorrow.

- Why had the search team rebuffed offers of help from the cell phone engineers?
- Had they relied too heavily on government search teams who didn't know the area and its confusing forest roads?
- What if Rachor had not delayed his search but began in earnest on December 2—the same day James Kim had left for help?

The only satisfying response to such gnawing questions is to face this tragedy's hard lessons. As one local wrote, "We can regret ourselves to heck and gone, and it won't change the past. Please, can't we do something to get people to stop using that route in bad weather? Maybe this can be our way to make it up to the family that James' legacy be that we do something to make sure no one else dies by making the mistake of taking that route in bad weather."[3]

Face the facts, review the mistakes—then change. Repent.

Repentance means, literally, to "re-think."[4] With the benefit of the big picture—including key players and their communications, conflicts, misguided emotions, and missed clues that cried for attention—only then can we truly re-think, learn, and change.

For example, hospital physicians systematically use "M&M" meetings to review their clinical errors. M&M stands for "morbidity and mortality," where unexpected deaths and complications are reviewed by one's medical peers with the goal of hospital-wide improvement. Hospitals have developed a system for encouraging all staff to face their errors and correct them. There is no hiding behind one's title or institutional clout—everyone's contribution to

---

3. Leslie C., Dec. 6, 2006, comment on Hunkins, "James Kim's Body."
4. Danker et al., "μετανοέω," *Greek-English Lexicon*, 567.

error is acknowledged and analyzed. The goal is not punishment but improvement of care.

The M&M is a tried-and-true map for serious—even deadly—mistakes.

THE EMOTIONS OF WRONGDOING

When we realize we've done something wrong, we may feel one of two emotions: *shame* or *guilt*.

Shame and guilt may seem similar, but their dynamics are profoundly different.

Shame is always about power—the power of a community to reject the wrongdoer, to shun and ostracize. The power to restore the wrongdoer rests in the hands of the community or some authority figure. Someone with power decides whether the wrongdoer is now acceptable and ready for "re-admission." And in today's social media world, that power can reside with an online mob or some vapid influencer.

What used to be the simple shame of local gossip is now intensified by social media.

The columnist David Brooks has noted that our modern culture has lost its shared understanding of right and wrong and has substituted shame.[5] Now, from high school kids to celebrities, neighbors to distant strangers, all are vulnerable to shaming on social media. A high school girl wears the same dress to a dance *and* a friend's bar mitzvah? Her double-duty dress will be ridiculed on Instagram. A neighbor doesn't pick up after his dog? He'll be roasted on Nextdoor's news feed. A politician erupts at her staff during a hectic day? Her character is skewered in the press, her presidential ambitions dashed.

And there is no clear way out of shame's wilderness. Shame's trails are always un-blazed; they're unpredictable and even unconscious. The shamed can internalize condemning voices and continually accuse their own selves, with no escape from those

---

5. Brooks, "Shame Culture."

inner voices. The shamers may feel unconsciously ashamed of something they've done in the past and project their shame onto others, indicting them for their own, secret crimes.

THE GOOD OF GUILT

There's a darkness in shame that keeps everyone lost in the wilderness—both the shamers and the shamed.

But guilt is different.

Guilt can launch us on a path to restoration and new life. Whether we've committed a public crime or a private sin, guilt sets in motion a sequenced path:

- Review: we face the full facts of our wrongdoing.
- Reflection: we reflect on why it happened.
- Restitution: we make amends for the wrong.
- Release: we ask forgiveness from those we've wronged.

These four steps make real repentance.

And notice this: these four steps are all within the power of the wrongdoer. They do not depend on anyone else's affirmation, acceptance, or approval. This is the crucial distinction between guilt and shame: guilt releases our personal power, but shame renders you powerless.

How does guilt give us power? When you feel guilt, you realize, "I can see the harm that I have done. And that awareness of what I've done comes from my own insight. So, with that agency and mindfulness, I have the tools to change."

"I see; I understand; I have agency; I have power."

Shame, in contrast, gives your power to the "mob." You just don't know what they'll do. Their actions are driven by capricious, even unconscious forces that are beyond your control.

Isn't the map of guilt so much better than the mob of shame?

FORGIVENESS

But what about forgiveness in this process? What about that fourth step of release, where we ask forgiveness from those we've wronged?

Doesn't forgiveness put power into the hands of another, who can withhold their forgiving word?

And, what if others' forgiveness just *cannot* come?

- Perhaps what you've done is secret and is better left concealed. Revealing it to others would only intensify injury.

- Perhaps, despite giving restitution, the injured party still won't forgive. In fact, it only further injures them when you ask for their forgiveness. "You've taken already a pound of flesh, and now you want my blood?"

Yet, even if others won't forgive us, there is no shortcut on this trail. We must follow its path of review to reflection, from reflection to restitution, and finally, from restitution to release—which comes only with forgiveness.

But for many, that final step of forgiveness won't or can't come from those you've wronged. What then?

FORGIVENESS FROM GOD

Here is where religion's power especially becomes clear. Because, for the religious, there is always another who can forgive. That other is God. Those who believe in God can count on God's forgiving love to complete their restoration.

But belief in God actually makes *more* of forgiveness in every way.

- Belief in God adds more realism to one's review of wrongdoing because we know that God sees us fully.

- Belief in God adds more depth to one's reflection on our motivations because we experience how God knows our hearts.

Eight Trails

- Belief in God adds more generosity to our restitution because we trust God's provision. Whatever we repay to the injured won't rob us of our true treasure—our dignity as God's child.
- Belief in God adds more renewal to our release because God promises to forgive fully.

BIBLICAL MAPS OF FORGIVENESS

The Bible is replete with stories and promises about the "more" of God's forgiveness.

- In the story of Jonah (and the whale), Jonah travels to the heathen city of Nineveh and calls on them to repent of their lives of sin. They do, which strangely embitters Jonah. God upbraids him and forgives Nineveh more than Jonah really wants.
- When Jesus utters his last words from the cross, he looks at his accusers and executioners and forgives them more than imaginable: "Father, forgive them, for they know not what they do" (Luke 23:34 ESV).
- In the Lord's Prayer, Jesus teaches us not only to pray for forgiveness, but he requires more of us, the forgiven: "Forgive us our trespasses *as we forgive those* who trespass against us."[6]

This is the power of forgiveness from God. Forgiveness from God is not transactional—it's not that I ask and God complies. It's more radical, more complete, and more demanding of us; it's truly transformational.

But this transformational move requires that we transform our beliefs. Belief in God can be a carefully considered symbolic choice about how we'll see our world.[7]

---

6. For the story of Jonah, see Jon 4; for the Lord's Prayer, see Matt 6:12.

7. I am speaking of "conversion" here as a carefully considered choice about how we'll symbolize our world and God. This choice will be discussed fully in this book's conclusion.

The Trail of Repentance

We can choose to believe that "the universe" is simply indifferent atoms and forces, that good and evil are just linguistic terms, and that our actions dissipate into nothing—nothing lost or gained.

Or we can choose to see the world as permeated with a loving personality: a "Father," a divine power that wants his world to manifest the good, the true, and the beautiful, that desires we align our lives with his personality and grow more like him daily.

And when we act against that in small or significant ways, he calls us to repent.

YOUR RATIONAL DECISION ABOUT REPENTANCE

Yes, you can recover from wrongdoing without belief in God. You can take hold of the four-step path of repentance without being religious. You can try to withstand our corrosive culture of shame, declaring you're deaf to its condemnations.

But walking this path *with God* puts you on a trail with more—more realism, more reflection, more restitution, more release for your repentance.

What will you choose? The capacity to progress in life absolutely depends upon repentance—facing our errors and ignorance and making essential change—not scapegoating others for our own wrongs, but facing ourselves bravely.

Will you walk this crucial path without religion, vulnerable to the crowd's shaming—or to your own inner critic?

Or will you walk with a God of infinite goodness who inspires your repentance?

CHAPTER 8

The Trail of Resurrection

PAPER CRANES FOR JAMES

James's memorial service was held at Golden Gate Park in San Francisco. His mourners created a stunning display of over a thousand paper cranes, each hand-folded in love and sympathy. Fluttering in the outdoor breeze and joyously colored, they were a fitting symbol for James's life.

But those cranes were more than a beautiful memento. Those familiar with Asian religions, including James's Korean family, would understand the deeper meaning of those cranes. Ancient Asian religions tell stories of cranes carrying the souls of the dead to paradise.

THE TRAIL OF RESURRECTION

As each of those mourners folded a paper crane, they were also folding into those cranes their own spiritual hopes for James—Nirvana, paradise, heaven, eternal life.

These hopes all point to a belief that there is existence beyond bodily death, a tenet of almost all religions. We'll consider this belief by its Christian name, "resurrection."

This is our final trail and destination.

THE BOOMERANG OF THE BEYOND

As we've considered each of the trails of life, we began with trails that seemed, at first glance, to need no religious faith to walk them. We looked at Rhythm, Relationship, and even Reverence as essential human experiences that one could "do" without religion.

But each new trail has taken us deeper into territory where spiritual understanding becomes more imperative. We have now walked some trails that can't be fully grasped without spiritual awareness—the trails of Revelation, Repentance, and especially now this: Resurrection.

I am going to use the word Resurrection in a very general way, without going into the details that divide religious groups and distinguish different faiths. Those details and debates arise when the focus is on the nature of an afterlife—is there a transitional zone like purgatory, are there heavenly angels, what about a final judgment, etc. But, as I've emphasized throughout this book, what's most important in religious life is less the details about these beliefs and more how they are used. Religious words, rituals, and other symbols do not just point to supernatural realities. The devout use these words, rituals, and symbols to "boomerang" back to them, shaping their action in the present.

That leads to an obvious observation: words and images about resurrection are used to shape our lives in this realm. We'll see that belief in an afterlife/heaven/resurrection has profound and positive consequences for this life.

AN AFTERLIFE? REALLY?

While engagement with institutional religion is on the decline, most Americans still believe in an afterdeath realm. According to the Roper Public Opinion Center at Cornell University, since 1945 the percentage of Americans who believe in life after death has remained almost the same: from 75 percent in 1945 when the question was first polled, to today's statistic of 73 percent.[1]

So, we're faced with a puzzle. People who have opted out of participation in traditional religious activities nonetheless persist in holding this religious belief!

Why would intelligent people believe in a reality that cannot be seen, measured, or verified by science? It must be, at *minimum*, that this belief has real consequences in *this* life. A belief in an afterlife must have a positive power for life today.

It provides a map for *today's* wilderness.

You've both asked me for prayers when your friends or their family were gravely ill—the aunt, the sorority sister, the newborn. And while not every prayer was answered with physical healing, the very act of prayer heals us, connecting us to the realm of the Healer, a greater power.

Prayer shows that no wilderness can shut out God, but *is* God's very temple.

SECULAR MAPS

People who have opted out of participation in traditional religious activities nonetheless persist in affirming an afterlife.

But what do those nonreligious folks *believe*?

One popular option could be the heaven described in books about near-death experiences. Beginning with the 1975 publication of Raymond Moody's book, *Life After Life*, accounts of near-death experiences (NDEs) have routinely become bestsellers. NDEs are characterized by testimonies about feeling peace, entering a realm

---

1. Roper Center, "Paradise Polled."

of light, communicating with other beings—and then returning to this life, usually in the midst of a medical emergency.

The prospect of a joyful afterlife might console us, but that points to the real problem of these NDEs. In this NDE type of heaven, all is bliss and light—no matter what you did in life, however evil or destructive. NDEs portray a heaven where what we've done *never* matters.

Belief in an NDE heaven is devoid of any moral implications for our life today.

So, in keeping with this inconsequential belief, we have inconsequential rituals. We have memorial services where there's hardly a whiff of religion—"celebrations of life" that are like a Rotary luncheon, with speakers honoring the deceased but no mention of God. No prayers are offered for the grieving, no calls are made for us to examine our souls, no reflections offered on eternal life and its meaning for today. Some religious songs might be sung, like "Amazing Grace," but their sacred references are washed out by the secular setting.

These are the hollow rites of the Church of NDEs.

If the validity of a map lies in how it guides our actions today, these NDE maps are—at best—mere sentimental consolation.

THE WILDERNESS AROUND THE CORNER

Here's a story, tragically too common, that demands a religious map.

As you were dressing for another day at school back in 2006, just around the corner, a crime was being discovered. A family had been murdered inside their own tidy, suburban home. By afternoon, it became public knowledge that the victims numbered a single mother and her two teenage sons, one a classmate of Erik's at Meadow Park Middle School.

Around three o'clock, you both came home. Siri reported that as classes ended at her grade school, the principal had announced over the intercom that the teachers were each to explain to their pupils about "what had happened."

Siri now looked at me and asked, "Mommy, Mrs. Hansen said there were no children killed. Right?"

My face crumbled. I could hardly get out the words and tell her the awful truth. And then came her next question: "Why?"

What would you tell a child, facing evil so close to home? "I'm sorry, dear, but bad things just sort of happen to nice people"? Would you say that "life is random and cruel"; that "children can be gunned down in their hallway, ending their lives too soon"; that "there is no final justice"?

I defy you to raise a child with such a worldview.

So, I spoke of our Christian faith in resurrection: "Siri, this is so horrible, so awful. But we believe in God and that God is love. We know God is caring for each of those kids right now. God is holding and healing them in heaven. And God will bring to judgment their killer. God will make this all come out right—in this life and in heaven."

This seemed to bring you some peace, based on your next question: "Mommy, can I have a snack?"

Believing in heaven came naturally for you kids. There were countless daily actions, rituals, and conversations that contributed to this belief. We went to church regularly; we had spiritually focused friends who held a special role in our lives; and we participated in small groups that read Scriptures and discussed how to apply them. We said table grace and nighttime prayers. We attended the funerals of church friends, where resurrection was preached and sung about.[2]

THE MOST IMPORTANT GAME

Through this Christian lifestyle, we weren't just engaged in some nice community. We were immersed in a "form of life," to adopt the language of Ludwig Wittgenstein. Our Christian form of life was (and continues to be) committed to Jesus as the highest

---

2. Religious sociologist Christian Smith has documented the power of family practices to transmit religious values and beliefs. See his books *Soul Searching* (with Melinda Lundquist Denton) and *Religious Parenting*.

exemplar of both human nature and God's character. Our daily dilemmas and special challenges are interpreted through the stories and teachings of Jesus to help us move ahead.

Wittgenstein called these regular patterns of words and action "language games." Although he used the phrase, "language game," these games are deadly serious. He called them "games" because a game has its own characteristic symbols and rules for using them. Through these "games," we solve real problems and find our way into the future.

So, just like there are a variety of games, with different playing pieces, rules, and goals, so too we practice a variety of games in everyday and professional life. Historians have their "game pieces" of historical documents and artifacts, and their rules for how to use them. Biologists have the game pieces of microscopic life and organic systems, and rules for how these are studied. And, as well, the religious have their game pieces of sacred wisdom, stories, and rituals, and how these are employed.[3]

---

3. Wittgenstein introduces that seminal phrase "language game" and describes the multiplicity of our language games in his book *Philosophical Investigations*.

"Here the term '*language-game*' is meant to bring into prominence the fact that the speaking of language is part of an activity, or of a *form of life*.
Review the multiplicity of language-games in the following examples, and in others:
Giving orders, and obeying them–
Describing the appearance of an object, or giving its measurements–
Constructing an object from a description (a drawing)–
Reporting an event–
Speculating about an event–
Forming and testing a hypothesis–
Presenting the results of an experiment in tables and diagrams–
Making up a story; and reading it–
Play-acting–
Guessing riddles–
Making a joke; telling it–
Solving a problem in practical arithmetic–
Translating from one language into another–
Asking, thinking, cursing, greeting, *praying*."

Wittgenstein, *Philosophical Investigations*, 11–12, para. 23; emphasis added.

But notice this. We are simultaneously biological and historical *and* spiritual beings, so we need all these language games.

THE LANGUAGE GAMES OF CARE

In our family's Christian "form of life," we weekly practiced our religious language game in Sunday worship, neighborhood conversation, religious readings, family prayers.

In particular, our church-based "Care Group" meetings were crucial in helping us become adept at the religious language game. There, we deeply discussed Scripture and its application to our lives.

When our group's leader, Jim Steinfeld, got brain cancer, our language game enabled us to face this crisis together.

We continually prayed for Jim's healing and the family's daily well-being.

But when Jim's suffering increased and we realized he would die, we didn't say, "Well, religion doesn't work! Those prayers were all for nothing." No, our Christian faith is based on Jesus Christ, who, himself, suffered and died. So, as Jim suffered and prepared to die, we prayed that he would sense Christ with him, sharing his suffering and fear.

As the Christian story unflinchingly records, as Jesus died on the cross, he cried, "My God, my God, why hast Thou forsaken me?" (Matt 27:46 KJV). And the Christian story recounts that God did not forsake him. God brought Christ through a harrowing death to eternal life.

Especially notice this. We didn't reject the language game of medical science in Jim's crisis. Members of our group were physicians and committed to medicine's power, and Jim himself tried every possible medical solution.

So, we moved between our language games—medicine and religion—seeking answers and help from each.

But the medical language game could only do so much. The religious language game, by contrast, gave us strength in each trying moment of sickness and crushing therapy. And our language game gave us hope, knowing Jim was united with Jesus Christ in eternal life.

CERTAINTY ABOUT HEAVEN

But why were we so confident that Jim was with Christ? How do we know eternal life is real? How can we be certain?

Jim was devoted to the teachings and spirit of Christ—that was the air he breathed. Your dad, John, remembers skiing with Jim on Mount Hood, setting out on a startlingly beautiful day of fresh snow and sunshine. As they rode the lift up, Jim said, "John, this place is so full of Christ's grace, blessing us with this day, let's just pray to him right now, thanking him for this moment."

Jim was already leaning into heaven because he saw heaven all around him. His vision of life—his Christian form of life—let him see the world as abounding in Christ.

His life was saturated by a reality—heaven—that can't be lost in death. Neither Christ's death nor Jim's.

Jesus linked confidence in heaven to our moral life in the present. In the Sermon on the Mount, he preached,

- "God blesses those people who depend only on him. They belong to the kingdom of heaven!" (Matt 5:3 NLT).
- "Blessed are those who are persecuted because of righteousness, for theirs is the kingdom of heaven" (Matt 5:10 NIV).
- "Blessed are you when people insult you, persecute you and falsely say all kinds of evil against you because of me. Rejoice and be glad, because great is your reward in heaven" (Matt 5:11–12 NIV).

Belief in heaven presses itself upon us as we live aligned with heaven's values. Every day we aspire to live by heavenly values. Then, over time and through circumstances that test us ("persecuted because of righteousness"), our conviction about heaven only grows because that is the world we inhabit.

The more one lives a "heavenly life," the more one believes in heaven! The moral integrity and joy of this form of life deepen belief in heaven.[4]

EVIL AND HEAVEN

But let's talk about that suffering and persecution that Jesus himself experienced—and taught us to not fear. What about the problem of evil—like those neighborhood murders?

Evil especially demands belief in an afterlife.

Philosopher and progenitor of the Enlightenment, Immanuel Kant observed that morally good people often suffered in this life because of their very goodness. Likewise, evil people frequently prospered and were not punished.[5]

The solution for Kant? He "postulated"[6] the existence of an afterlife.[7] Only in such an afterlife could the good person experience

---

4. I am indebted to the insight of Paul Holmer's, "On Believing in Heaven."

5. "Now it is clear . . . that the maxims of virtue and those of private happiness are quite heterogeneous as to their supreme practical principle, and, although they belong to one summum bonum which together they make possible, yet they are so far from coinciding that they restrict and check one another very much in the same subject. Thus the question: 'How is the summum bonum practically possible?' still remains an unsolved problem." Kant, *Critique of Practical Reason*, 1.2.2 (§113).

6. "The summum bonum, then, practically is only possible on the supposition of the immortality of the soul; consequently this immortality, being inseparably connected with the moral law, is *a postulate of pure practical reason* (by which I mean *a theoretical proposition, not demonstrable* as such, but which is an inseparable result of an unconditional a priori practical law)."Kant, *Critique of Practical Reason*, 1.2.4 (§123); emphasis added.

7. "*In respect, then, of the holiness which the Christian law requires, this leaves the creature nothing but a progress in infinitum*, but for that very reason it justifies him in hoping for an endless duration of his existence. The worth of a character perfectly accordant with the moral law is infinite, since the only restriction on all possible happiness in the judgement of a wise and all powerful distributor of it is the absence of conformity of rational beings to their duty. But the moral law of itself does not promise any happiness, for according to our conceptions of an order of nature in general, this is not necessarily connected with obedience to the law. Now Christian morality supplies this defect

The Trail of Resurrection

the joy they deserve.[8] Universal reason demands that—somehow, some "where," in some "time"—the good are rewarded.

We postulate, we construct, we *believe* that reward must come through this "thing" called "heaven."

But please note this: Kant argued that we should do good not in order to gain heavenly happiness, but because good is right to do! Indeed, we do good *despite* the possibility that it might make us unhappy today. But in the afterlife realm, we will experience that happiness of which we are worthy.

And so it is, likewise, for punishment. Those who have escaped earthly punishment for evil will now experience divine consequences in an afterlife. Again, we're not going to quibble about the details of various afterlife beliefs. But almost all religions are united in believing in judgment of all and justice for victims.

You kids witnessed the abrupt and unjust dismissal I suffered, orchestrated by a few church leaders. You and so many were outraged—many even withdrew from the church. But don't withdraw from God! I counted on God's justice, not human justice, and in that promise I found peace for moving forward. As Prov 29:26 reminds us, "Many seek the face of a ruler, but it is from the Lord that a man gets justice."

(of the second indispensable element of the summum bonum) by representing the world in which rational beings devote themselves with all their soul to the moral law, as a kingdom of God, in which nature and morality are brought into a harmony foreign to each of itself, by a holy Author who makes the derived summum bonum possible. Holiness of life is prescribed to them as a rule even in this life, while the welfare proportioned to it, namely, *bliss, is represented as attainable only in an eternity*; because the former must always be the pattern of their conduct in every state, and progress towards it is already possible and necessary in this life; while the latter, under the name of *happiness, cannot be attained at all in this world* (so far as our own power is concerned), and therefore is made simply an object of hope." Kant, *Critique of Practical Reason*, 1.2.5 (§129); emphasis added.

8. Kant didn't see the afterlife as a zone of heavenly reward, but rather a realm of "infinite progress," where our immortal souls keep on progressing toward a moral perfection not possible in this life. I wonder if Kant's realm of infinite progress is much like the Mormon doctrine of heaven, where souls continue their sanctification toward becoming *like* their heavenly parent.

The upshot? We must construct a map whose edges extend beyond our mortal lives. Those extended "edges" keep us striving for the good. That map keeps us from becoming discouraged from doing the right thing. It keeps us from becoming evil ourselves to avenge unpunished wrongs.

Religions around the world have formulated their own constructions of this map through their stories, rituals, and teachings. The map is used by their followers to inspire their moral action.

These maps lift all humanity by supporting good deeds today and justice in the future.

YOUR RATIONAL CHOICE ABOUT RESURRECTION

Yes, you can believe in some vague afterlife without having a religion. You can try to persevere and do the right thing without expecting a heavenly reward.

But we all will someday face a dark wilderness of suffering and death and its challenge to life's meaning. Children will be murdered; a faith leader will die of cancer; good people will suffer injustice no human court can correct.

Those who don't believe in God must use maps supplied by popular thought:

- Hope for some vague, heavenly realm where everyone "gets in."
- Living in the moment without concern for the soul we're building—or destroying.
- No confidence that doing good leaves a lasting legacy.
- A life divided starkly between the "now" and a vague "hereafter" that barely enters our thoughts.

Religions' maps are so much clearer. Their distinct and tested maps sustain us when life seems cruel and unfair. Their moral lines can guide our way through the darkest of life's trails. They shine the light of heaven on our walk in this harsh wilderness.

What will you choose?

CHAPTER 9

Conclusion

CHOOSE YOUR MAP, CHOOSE YOUR FAITH

Each trail in this book has been framed as a choice—what "map" will you use to traverse life's trails? I've framed the choice in general terms, as a choice between religious faith and secularism.

If you've made it this far in our journey, however, my hunch is you're drawn to the religious option (or you're just a loyal family reader).

But one can't be religious "generally." The effectiveness of any faith needs grounding in a community of fellow believers. In the introduction, I advised you to find experienced fellow adventurers to help you read your maps and understand how to follow their symbols.

That is, find a religious community.

Eight Trails

IS RELIGION REALLY A CHOICE?

But, can you even *choose* a religion rationally?

In the history of religion and philosophy, many have thought otherwise:

- Some see this choice as a passionate "leap of faith," as Søren Kierkegaard put it[1]—a commitment based not on rational knowledge, but passionate obedience to God.
- Some insist this process is beyond your control, where the Spirit enters and transforms your soul, making you "born-again."
- Some argue you're simply opting for one of many worldviews, each an insular bubble with its own truths and values, as relativism argues.

You might guess where I am. If I thought religious choice were merely an irrational leap, a miraculous rebirth, or an impenetrable bubble, I wouldn't have written this book.

This book presupposes that there is a rational process that undergirds this momentous commitment:

- even when that decision seems like a leap, made with limited knowledge. After all, by any definition of "God," no one can fully know God. So, we take a leap, *rationally* accepting the limits of our knowledge.
- even when that decision seems Spirit-controlled. After all, we wouldn't say yes to a spirit that commanded evil. So, *rationally*, we judge the character of the spirit that's stirring within.
- even when another's religion seems so strange, it feels wrong to evaluate it, let alone claim understanding. Yet, we implicitly evaluate religions by *rationally observing* the culture and character each engenders and making judgments about that.

In short, as you consider your commitment, religious discernment is *rational*.

---

1. Kierkegaard, *Concluding Unscientific Postscript*, 335.

CONCLUSION

FIRST COMES "NO"

Kids, you've declared your own "no" over the years, having observed the meanness, dishonesty, and fearful conformity of some churches that we've known.

So, let's look at some people, like yourself, whose own rational discernment begins with rejection—of a faith tradition, a single church, or a religious lifestyle. Finally, we'll note that there are secularists—some quite famous—who now say no to life *without* religion.

As I write this conclusion, religion is in the news. For the first time since the American Enterprise Institute (AEI) began sponsoring regular surveys, it now documents young women leaving churches in numbers that outstrip men's leaving.

This has never happened before! Men have, statistically, been much more inclined to leave a church, while women have stayed.

What's going on? The AEI study concluded,

> For most young women who leave it's not about any one issue.... Rather it was a steady accumulation of negative experiences and dissonant teachings that made it difficult or impossible to stay. Much of this dissonance stems from growing up in a culture that has become more diverse and accepting of people with distinctive lifestyles and identities.[2]

These women are making a rational choice to reject the worldview of their churches. Their sense of dissonance arises from their modern life with its facts and values. And notice this: these women aren't living in some religious bubble. They live in a world where their church's worldview and their public life intersect at crucial junctures.

We can see that rational, religious discernment in the life of Rachel Held Evans. Rachel was a beloved, influential voice for many American Evangelicals who were uneasy in their churches.[3] Her book *A Year of Biblical Womanhood* chronicled her at-

---

2. Cox and Hammond, "Young Women."
3. Held Evans suffered an untimely death at thirty-seven, apparently from

tempt to live for one year following the Bible's dictates literally. It exposed—often hilariously—that demands to live "biblically" can be hollow rhetoric. Rather, a real biblical faith requires going past literalism with a thoughtful, figurative grasp of Scripture.

This experience sowed seeds of further dissonance with Rachel's evangelical world. Her break from her longtime church finally came when its leaders explicitly called the congregation to "Vote Yes On One," a state ballot initiative to limit legal marriage to heterosexual couples.

Rachel wrote,

> I have friends who struggled for years to disentangle themselves from abusive, authoritarian churches where they were publicly shamed for asking questions and thinking for themselves. I know of others who were kicked out for getting divorced or for being gay. These are important stories to tell, but they are not mine. I left a church of kind, generous people because I couldn't pretend to believe things I didn't believe anymore, because no matter how hard I tried, I could never be the stick-figured woman in the *Vote Yes On One* sign, standing guard in front of the doors.[4]

SURPRISING NOS

And such religious dissonance isn't limited to American evangelical women, with modern work lives and internet access. On the other side of the globe, in Iran, a similar dissonance is felt by many Muslim women. In 2022, an Iranian woman was jailed for wearing her headscarf askew and then was beaten to death by her jailers. Iranian women took to the streets in brave protest, demanding justice and the lifting of oppressive rules on women.[5]

---

encephalitis. Graham, "Rachel Held Evans."
    4. Evans, *Searching for Sunday*, 164.
    5. Krauss, "What Kept Iran Protests."

CONCLUSION

A thoughtful, rational reflection undergirds these choices of "no." Relying on observation, intuition, and education that burst the supposed bubble of their religion, these women are saying no!

But, one can also say no to a secular life. We're now seeing surprising affirmations of religious life from once adamant atheists: Paul Kingsnorth, Tom Holland, Jordan Peterson, and Terry Eagleton, even Richard Dawkins, famous for his book *The God Delusion*.[6]

Elizabeth Oldfield documents that shift in a recent article:

> Whereas the New Atheists rejected religion because the Bible didn't read like a science textbook, those now feeling the pull of the church are driven by "the meaning crisis." ... Beset by existential angst, they hunger for a story in which to orient themselves. Take Jordan Peterson, the Canadian psychologist and cultural commentator. ... He, and those under his influence, praise Christianity for its imaginative resources—its myth and ritual, its moral clarity.[7]

Your religious journey of rational discernment, in short, may begin with a no.

But how do you get to yes?

HOW NOT TO SAY YES

The premise of *Eight Trails* is that religious stories, doctrines, and rituals work like maps. These maps' purpose has always been to orient believers about how to live—how to "hike" the uncertain trails of life.

The validity of a religion, then, is how well its maps help its believers live. What kind of life is engendered by these maps?

That's how we'll get to yes—*that's how we'll choose a religious tradition and its local community.*

---

6. Caldwell, "Cultural Christian."
7. Oldfield, "Secular Figures."

Eight Trails

Can you appreciate how very different this is from the way some choose their religion?

- Some choose a faith based not on its outcomes but on its supernatural origins. They are persuaded that a religion is true because it was *revealed by a supernatural source*—God spoke to Moses, the angel Gabriel spoke to Muhammad, the resurrected Christ to the apostle Paul, two glorious "personages" to Joseph Smith, etc.

- Some will claim that their sacred literature is true because its stories are historically true, corroborated by witnesses. For example, this is the claim of those who insist that the four Gospel accounts of Jesus were written by eyewitnesses, who recorded their observations without error or contradiction.

- Some will claim that their religion's metaphysical doctrines (teachings about the origin and destiny of the world) are true because they correlate with scientific discovery—or will someday. We see this correlation move in religions that are eager to reconcile their doctrines with each new scientific theory or discovery, such as the big bang, evolution, the "God" particle, etc.

Yet, do you see how fraught these foundations are?

- In the first case—supernatural origins—a religion's claim to truth amounts to nothing more than the claims of its *insiders*. Here we are asked to accept that God spoke to *their* founding prophets, and to them alone revealed "the truth."

- In the second and third cases, the validity of religion rests on the work of those *outside* of a faith—historians, archaeologists, scientists, etc. whom believers hope will confirm their faith. However, anyone who understands such fields knows their findings and theories may change with new data. (And anyone familiar with religion knows that no new data *ever* is seen to refute a core religious belief.[8])

---

8. Ludwig Wittgenstein made this point several times in his "Lectures on

CONCLUSION

No, we can't choose a religion based on insider claims about its origins or outsider tests of verification. That way *undermines* any religion's claim to truth.

The only way forward is practical and public: we test the maps of a religious faith. How well does a faith help its followers find their way on life's trails?

As my mentor, Harvard theologian Gordon Kaufman, wrote, "Of proposed concepts of *God* . . . therefore, one must ask such questions as these: What forms of life do these conceptions facilitate? Which forms inhibit? What possibilities do they open up for men and women? Which do they close off?"[9]

SAY YES—TO GOD

I hope you're now seeing religious choice as a matter of rational discernment. One must weigh a faith's capacity to help you walk life's Eight Trails.

But what about God? Is this choice all about the trail, looking down at your feet? What about looking "up" at God?

Looking "down at your feet" is a clear, straightforward assessment. It doesn't take a leap of faith or mystical rebirth to commit to a religion's *way of life*.

But, what about believing in the *god* who is central to that religion? That's, frankly, less straightforward. And some people think it's optional. We've seen lately those who insist that they endorse the ideals and practices of a religion, but they don't believe in its god. They consider themselves a "cultural Christian" or a "cultural Muslim" or a "cultural Hindu" without believing in its deity.

Yet, "God" is the central symbol of any religious tradition. A religion's symbolization of God impacts its moral code, its

---

Religious Belief," citing as evidence that while believers may *seem* to use historical or scientific terms in their faith, in fact, they are using such terms differently than the practitioners of history and science. They are playing a different "language game" (Wittgenstein's famous term) with different goals and criteria than science or history. See Wittgenstein, *Lectures and Conversations*, 53–72.

9. Kaufman, *Essay on Theological Method*, 32.

understanding of the world, its vision of the future, and its teaching about life's stakes.

The symbol for God "presides" over a religion's entire symbol system. It sets the boundaries, so to speak, of a religious way of life. For example, a god who is characterized by its scriptures as "love" creates essential boundaries against those who would claim their faith allows them to practice hate. Religious leaders may try to call on believers to do terrible things in "God's name." But believers will start to sense that crucial boundaries are being violated, distorting the very identity of their god.

GOD WITH A SMALL "G"

To be a cultural believer—setting aside God as "optional"—can endanger the very culture valued by the cultural believer.

But most importantly, those who affirm a religion's symbolic richness (its culture) but dismiss its god, show they don't understand that *God is also a symbol.*

Throughout the Eight Trails, we've asked you to think about religion in a new way, reframing it as a rich collection of maps. This "map" reframing applies to God, as well (see the introduction and chapter 2).

In speaking about God as a map, we're acknowledging that our knowledge and interaction with God always occur through symbols—through stories, rituals, artistic works, abstract concepts, and detailed doctrines. I've been calling these symbols "maps."

Without our maps—our religious symbols—there is no encounter with God!

Is this a demotion of some kind? I'll answer: it's not a demotion of God. But it is a demotion of our *pretensions* to know God "face-to-face," free of any symbols.

The Harvard philosopher Hilary Putnam made a useful distinction here that we could adopt. Putnam often characterized himself as a philosophical realist. Still, he refused to fall into the pretension that we can know objective reality—reality without our interpretive symbols, schemes, and concepts.

Conclusion

Rather, Putnam championed being a realist, but *with a small "r."* That is, we deal with the realities of science, history, and everyday life through the symbol systems we have built up for each. Thus, Putnam taught, we don't have access to some (capital R) Reality. But we have access to reality with a small "r"—and that lets us get on with life![10]

That's the choice before you. Can you commit to *God with a small "g"*?

It won't be God with a capital "G", but this god is good enough! To paraphrase another philosopher, "Enough is good enough, even though enough isn't everything!"[11]

Moreover—and this is a crucial point—*the world's great religious traditions all regard their knowledge of God with a small "g."*

- In Hinduism, the ultimate unknowability of God is expressed through the symbol of Brahman. Brahman is considered the ultimate reality, yet beyond human comprehension.

- In Zen Buddhism, the ultimate nature of reality is taught as fundamentally unknowable through intellectual or discursive means. The Heart Sutra famously states, "Form is emptiness, emptiness is form," pointing to the ineffable nature of ultimate reality.

- In Judaism, the unknowability of God is reflected in the prohibition of making images of God. Even speaking God's name is prohibited, so it's written without vowels (YHWH). The Torah emphasizes that God is beyond human comprehension

---

10. See Hilary Putnam's autobiographical note on his phrase "realism with a small 'r'" in Putnam, "Replies," 353.

11. Hilary Putnam quotes philosopher John Austin, "Enough is enough, even though enough isn't everything," in Putnam, *Realism*, 121–22, 131. Gordon Kaufman made a similar point about a symbol-mediated reality and God being "good enough": "All human concepts of reality are constructs which have significance for us to the degree that they provide us with useful maps for dealing with life; none can be checked in some extra-pragmatic way to see whether they 'correspond' to 'reality.' *If we realize what is involved in such all-comprehensive concepts, we will not expect more.*" Kaufman, *Essay on Theological Method*, 76; emphasis added.

and description, often referred to as "Eyn Sof" (the Infinite) or simply as "HaShem" (the Name).

- In Islam, the Qur'an repeatedly asserts that God is beyond human understanding and comprehension, emphasizing divine transcendence and incomparability. Islamic theologians and mystics, such as those in the Sufi tradition, often speak of "veils" that obscure direct knowledge of God.

- In both the Old and New Testaments of the Christian Bible, the ultimate unknowability of God is a recurring theme. Isaiah 55:8–9 declares, "For my thoughts are not your thoughts, neither are your ways my ways," declares the Lord. "For as the heavens are higher than the earth, so are my ways higher than your ways and my thoughts than your thoughts." Similarly, 1 Tim 6:16 states, "God dwells in unapproachable light, whom no one has ever seen or can see."

Belief in God with a small "g" has stood the test of time and tradition. It is good enough for the world's great faiths.

Is it now good enough for you?

THE MAP THAT MOVES YOUR EMOTIONS

I've been making the case for rational reflection in your religious discernment and commitment.

But now, it's time to consider our emotions.

Throughout this book, I've invited you to consider the power of maps from the world's great religions: their stories, doctrines, rituals, and music—their symbols. These symbols, used wisely, have the power to help us face our greatest challenges, reshape lost and broken people, and savor life's sublime beauty.

When these life-giving symbols touch you, you may feel awe, gratitude, reverence, and trust. But these feelings are not so much for the symbols—after all, they're "just" maps—but for the God you glimpse *through* the symbols.

God can evoke our deepest emotions.

CONCLUSION

Yes, God helps us make sense of our world, rationally. Our symbols for God manage to take all the complexity of life, the vast unknown of the cosmos, and the uncertainty about the future, and compress these overwhelming facts and questions into a map that orients us. Now we can sense our "location"—our metaphysical situation.

But God doesn't simply map a metaphysical world. God maps an emotional world. For this is a map of our *home*—our existential home. One of the most emotionally charged experiences of life is home. And the host of this home is *God*.

Now, our rational discernment of religion is joined by the deepest emotions—love, devotion, worship for God. And these emotions are not superfluous or expendable. They especially enable us to follow the map. To follow the trails of life with God, we need these powerful emotions!

So, along with your rational discernment of the forms of life afforded by different faiths, now factor in the emotions evoked by their respective gods.

- What is God's "personality" in each religious tradition?
- Can you love and *follow* that personality?
- Does that personality promise you safety, yet inspire brave service to others?

Use your emotions as your final but critical form of intelligence as you make your religious commitment.

NEXT STEPS!

To summarize our consideration of religion, now join emotion with your reason.

- Emotion: choose a religious community based on the lives it lifts and rescues. Reason: examine its real-life *ethics*.

- Emotion: choose a religion whose vision of the world inspires your wonder and stewardship. Reason: question its *metaphysics*.
- Emotion: choose a religion whose God fills you with love and trust. Reason: be tough-minded about its *theology*.

Choose a religion, my kids, with all your *mind and heart*.
Then boldly hike your Eight Trails.

Love,
Mom

Bibliography

Austin, David, and Mark Larabee. "On the Road, a Family Vanishes: Southern Oregon Is the Focus of a Search for a Couple and Their Children, Missing After a Portland Stop." *The Oregonian*, Dec. 2, 2006.

Babcock, Maltbie D. "This Is My Father's World." In *Sing Joyfully*, #40. Carol Stream, IL: Tabernacle, 1989. https://hymnary.org/text/this_is_my_fathers_world_and_to_my.

Bass, Dorothy. *Practicing Our Faith: A Way of Life for a Searching People.* San Francisco, CA: Jossey-Bass, 1997.

Baumeister, Roy F., et al. *Losing Control: How and Why People Fail at Self-Regulation.* San Diego, CA: Academic Press, 1994.

Brooks, David. "The Shame Culture." *New York Times*, Mar. 15, 2016. https://www.nytimes.com/2016/03/15/opinion/the-shame-culture.html.

Brown, Brené. *Rising Strong.* New York: Spiegel & Grau, 2015.

Buber, Martin. *I and Thou.* Translated by Ronald Gregor Smith. Edinburgh: T&T Clark, 1937.

Caldwell, Simon. "'I'm a Cultural Christian,' Declares Richard Dawkins, the World's Most Famous Atheist." *Catholic Herald*, Apr. 5, 2024. https://thecatholicherald.com/im-a-cultural-christian-declares-richard-dawkins-the-worlds-most-famous-atheist/.

Capra, Frank, dir. *It's a Wonderful Life.* New York: RKO Radio Pictures, 1947.

Case, Anne, and Angus Deaton. *Deaths of Despair and the Future of Capitalism.* Princeton: Princeton University Press, 2020.

Cassirer, Ernest. *An Essay on Man.* New Haven: Yale University Press, 1944.

Chödrön, Pema. *No Time to Lose: A Timely Guide to the Way of the Bodhisattva.* Boulder, CO: Shambhala, 2005.

Cox, Daniel A., and Kelsey Eyre Hammond. "Young Women Are Leaving Church in Unprecedented Numbers." Survey Center on American Life, Apr. 4, 2024. https://www.americansurveycenter.org/newsletter/young-women-are-leaving-church-in-unprecedented-numbers/.

Danker, Frederick W., et al, eds. *Greek-English Lexicon of the New Testament and Other Early Christian Literature.* 3rd ed. Chicago: University of Chicago Press, 2000.

Emerson, Ralph Waldo. *Nature and Selected Essays.* Edited by Larzer Ziff. London: Penguin, 2003.

Evans, Rachel Held. *Searching for Sunday.* Nashville: Nelson, 2015.

Fagan, Patrick F. "Adolescent Hard Drug Use By Family Structure and Religious Practice." Marriage and Religion Research Institute. https://marri.us/wp-content/uploads/MA-7-9-151.pdf.

Fagan, Patrick F., and Althea Nagai. "Children with a Learning Disability By Family Structure and Religious Practice." Marriage and Religion Research Institute. https://marri.us/wp-content/uploads/MA-141.pdf.

———. "Divorce or Separation in Adulthood by Family Structure and Religious Practice During Adolescence." Marriage and Religion Research Institute. https://marri.us/wp-content/uploads/MA-61-63-169.pdf.

———. "Drinks Too Much Alcohol By Family Structure and Religious Practice." Marriage and Religion Research Institute. https://marri.us/wp-content/uploads/MA-85-87-177.pdf.

———. "Feels Thrilled, Excited During Sexual Intercourse By Family Structure and Religious Practice." Marriage and Religion Research Institute. https://marri.us/wp-content/uploads/MA-116.pdf.

———. "Marital Happiness by Family Structure and Religious Practice." Marriage and Religion Research Institute. https://marri.us/wp-content/uploads/MA-31-33-159.pdf.

———. "Work Fulfillment By Family Structure and Religious Practice." Marriage and Religion Research Institute. https://marri.us/wp-content/uploads/MA-76-78-174.pdf.

Fideler, David. *Breakfast with Seneca.* New York: Norton, 2022.

Graham, Ruth. "Rachel Held Evans, the Hugely Popular Christian Writer Who Challenged the Evangelical Establishment, Is Dead at 37." Slate, Mar. 4, 2019. https://slate.com/human-interest/2019/05/rachel-held-evans-the-hugely-popular-evangelical-writer-is-dead-at-37.html.

Hamilton, Jon. "Orphans' Lonely Beginnings Reveal How Parents Shape a Child's Brain." NPR, Feb. 24, 2014. https://www.npr.org/sections/health-shots/2014/02/20/280237833/orphans-lonely-beginnings-reveal-how-parents-shape-a-childs-brain.

Hawks, Annie S. "The Angel of the Lord." In *The Cyber Hymnal*, edited by Dick Adams, #9334. HymnTime.com. Accessed on Hymnary.org. https://hymnary.org/text/be_still_my_doubting_soul.

Holmer, Paul. "On Believing in Heaven." *Pietisten* 5 (1990). http://www.pietisten.org/v/1/on_believing.html.

Horwitz, Ilana M. "I Followed the Lives of 3,290 Teenagers. This Is What I Learned About Religion and Education." *New York Times*, Mar. 15, 2022. https://www.nytimes.com/2022/03/15/opinion/religion-school-success.html.

Huber, J. Parker. "John Muir's Menu." *Sierra* 79.6 (1994). https://vault.sierraclub.org/john_muir_exhibit/life/john_muir_menu_j_parker_huber.aspx.

BIBLIOGRAPHY

Hulme, T. E. "Romanticism and Classicism." Poetry Foundation, Feb. 14, 2010. https://www.poetryfoundation.org/articles/69477/romanticism-and-classicism.

Humphreys, Kathryn L., et al. "Effects of Institutional Rearing and Foster Care on Psychopathology at Age 12 Years in Romania: Follow-Up of an Open, Randomised Controlled Trial." *The Lancet Psychiatry* 2 (2015) 625–34. https://www.thelancet.com/journals/lanpsy/article/PIIS2215-0366(15)00095-4/abstract.

Hunkins, Joe. "James Kim's Body Found in Rogue River Wilderness." JoeDuck (blog), Dec. 6, 2006. https://joeduck.com/2006/12/06/james-kim-search/.

James, William. *The Varieties of Religious Experience*. Transcript of lecture delivered at the Gifford Lectures on Natural Religion, Edinburgh, 1902. Edited and annotated by LeRoy L. Miller. https://www.truthunity.net/books/william-james-the-varieties-of-religious-experience.

Kant, Immanuel. *The Critique of Practical Reason*. Translated by J. M. D. Meiklejohn. Great Books of the Western World 42. Chicago: Chicago University Press, 1952.

Kaufman, Gordon. *An Essay on Theological Method*. Missoula, MT: Scholars, 1979.

Kierkegaard, Søren. *Concluding Unscientific Postscript to Philosophical Fragments*. Translated by Howard V. Hong and Edna H. Hong. Princeton: Princeton University, 1992.

King, Dean. *Guardians of the Valley: John Muir and the Friendship That Saved Yosemite*. New York: Scribner, 2023.

Krauss, Joseph. "Explainer: What Kept Iran Protests Going After First Spark?" AP, Sept. 21, 2022. https://apnews.com/article/iran-protests-morality-police-explainer-b53475eda867a4158ac5032fe1b3e62e.

Kuhn, Thomas. *The Structure of Scientific Revolutions*. Chicago: University of Chicago Press, 1962.

Lambert, Nathaniel M., and David C. Dollahite. "How Religiosity Helps Couples Prevent, Resolve, and Overcome Marital Conflict." *Family Relations* 55 (2006) 439–49. https:/brightspotcdn.byu.edu/b6/e2/f6f0e65540848fe6e991b5052c05/s-40howreligiositylambertdollahite2006pdf.pdf.

Lednicer, Lisa Grace. "Following a Hunch, Pilot Finds Kati Kim." *The Oregonian*, Dec. 8, 2006.

Lewis, C. S. *Miracles: A Preliminary Study*. New York: HarperOne, 1996.

Marri. "Marriage and Family." https://marri.us/marriage-and-family/.

Mohr, Joseph. "Silent Night, Holy Night." In *Sing Joyfully*, #189. Carol Stream, IL: Tabernacle, 1989. https://hymnary.org/text/silent_night_holy_night_all_is_calm_all.

Oldfield, Elizabeth. "Secular Figures Are Giving Faith a Second Look." *Christianity Today* 67.8 (Nov. 2023). https://www.christianitytoday.com/2023/10/surprising-rebirth-belief-god-justin-brierley/.

Piaget, Jean. *Science of Education and the Psychology of the Child*. Translated by Derek Coltman. New York: Orion, 1970.

Piff, Paul, and Dacher Keltner. "Why Do We Experience Awe?" *New York Times*, May 22, 2015. https://www.nytimes.com/2015/05/24/opinion/sunday/why-do-we-experience-awe.html?referrer&_r=5.

Putnam, Hilary. *Realism with a Human Face*. Cambridge: Harvard University Press, 1992.

———. "Replies." *Philosophical Topics* 20 (1992) 347–408. http://www.jstor.org/stable/43154648.

Rede, George. "Kati Kim Speaks Out in OregonLive Comments About Surviving 2006 Oregon Wilderness Tragedy." *Oregonian*, Jan. 22, 2011. https://www.oregonlive.com/news/2011/01/kati_kim_speaks_out_on_oregonl.html.

Riopel, Leslie. "Resilience Examples: What Key Skills Make You Resilient?" Positive Psychology, Jan. 20, 2019. https://positivepsychology.com/resilience-skills/.

Robbins, Mel. "No One Is Coming (It's Up to You)." YouTube, Apr. 18, 2024. https://www.youtube.com/watch?v=fAXgU-fcr-Q.

Robbins, Tony. "The 20 Best Motivational Quotes." Tony Robbins (website). https://www.tonyrobbins.com/tony-robbins-quotes/inspirational-quotes.

Roberts, Michelle. "Kati Kim Retraces Tragic Journey." *The Oregonian*, Jan. 19, 2007.

Roper Center. "Paradise Polled: Americans and the Afterlife." June 15, 2005. https://ropercenter.cornell.edu/paradise-polled-americans-and-afterlife.

Schleiermacher, Friedrich. *On Religion: Speeches to Its Cultured Despisers*. 2nd ed. Translated and edited by Richard Crouter. Cambridge: Cambridge University Press, 1996.

Smith, Christian, and Melinda Lundquist Denton. *Soul Searching: The Religious and Spiritual Lives of American Teenagers*. Oxford: Oxford University Press, 2005.

Smith, Christian, et al. *Religious Parenting: Transmitting Faith and Values in Contemporary America*. Princeton: Princeton University Press, 2019.

Smith, James K. A. *You Are What You Love*. Grand Rapids: Brazos, 2016.

Smith, Peter. "Church Agency: Captive Missionaries Made Daring Escape." Assocaited Press, Dec. 20, 2021. https://apnews.com/article/kidnapping-haiti-9eb3ebd8f3c2c268dad5e0cc68d6135a.

Spurgeon, Charles. "Brave Waiting." Sermon delivered on Aug. 26, 1877. Spurgeon Center. https://www.spurgeon.org/resource-library/sermons/brave-waiting/#flipbook/.

Suh, Elizabeth, and David Austin. "Kim Likely Dead 2 Days Before Body Found." *The Oregonian*, Dec. 8, 2006.

Suo, Steve, and Elizabeth Suh. "Kim Case Reveals Gap in Search Know-How." *The Oregonian*, Jan. 20, 2007.

Suo, Steve, et al. "Conflicts, Confusion Undermine Search." *The Oregonian*, Jan. 19, 2007.

BIBLIOGRAPHY

Sykes, Christopher, ed. *No Ordinary Genius. The Illustrated Richard Feynman.* New York: Norton, 1996.

Troyer, David. "Hostages Freed." Christian Aid Ministries, Dec. 17, 2021. https://christianaidministries.org/haiti-kidnapping-update/haiti-staff-abduction/.

Wayland, Francis. "Case of Conviction." *American Baptist Magazine*, Oct. 1831. https://www.merrycoz.org/articles/WAYLAND.xhtml.

Wettstein, Howard K. *The Significance of Religious Experience.* Oxford: Oxford University Press, 2012.

Winnicott, D. W. "The Theory of the Parent-Infant Relationship." *International Journal of Psychoanalysis* 41 (1960) 585–95.

Wittgenstein, Ludwig. *Lectures and Conversations on Aesthetics, Psychology and Religious Belief.* Edited by Cyril Barrett. Oakland, CA: University of California Press, 1967.

———. *Philosophical Investigations.* Translated by G. E. M. Anscombe. Oxford: Basil Blackwell, 1986.

Young, Molly. "Better Living Through Stoicism, from Seneca to Modern Interpreters." *New York Times*, Dec. 28, 2021. https://www.nytimes.com/2021/12/28/books/stoicism-books.html.

www.ingramcontent.com/pod-product-compliance
Lightning Source LLC
Chambersburg PA
CBHW072200100426
42738CB00011BA/2483